How I Made $10 Million From Internet Affiliate Marketing

ANTOINE WALKER

Visit my website at:

http://www.dotaffiliate.com

Copyright

Copyright © 2012 by Antoine Walker

All Rights Reserved

No part of this book may be reproduced in any form or by any electronic or mechanical means including information storage and retrieval systems—except in the case of brief quotations in articles or reviews—without the permission in writing from its publisher, Antoine Walker.

All brand names and product names used in this book are trademarks, registered trademarks, or trade names of their respective holders. We are not associated with any product or vendor in this book.

ISBN-10: 1479291986
ISBN-13: 978-1479291984

DEDICATION

This book is dedicated to the people who stood by me during the court proceedings. You know who you are.

This book is also dedicated to the special people who are currently in my life

CONTENTS

1	Introduction	1
2	What is Affiliate Marketing?	3
3	The Beginning	5
4	Yahoo Auctions	7
5	All Advantage	10
6	My Last Regular Job	14
7	The Real Money	19
8	Crazy New Ideas	22
9	Charity	34
10	Obsessed	37
11	Omega Sex?	39
12	Getting Big Fast	42
13	Burnout	55
14	Search Engines	57
15	Employee Incompetence	62
16	The Software Won't Work	64
17	Finding Advertisers	66
18	Lake Tahoe	73
14	Locked Out	75
15	Justice?	78

16	Starting From Scratch	80
17	Search Engine Optimization	82
18	Moving On	88
19	Taxes	92
20	Poker Forum	100
21	Private Labeling	103
22	The Power of a Dollar	105
23	A Big Move	109
24	Geotargetting	111
25	Domain Names	113
26	Charity Revisited	118
27	Values	123
28	Investments	126
29	My Current Recipe	128
30	Penguins	134
31	Affiliate Programs	136
32	Coming Full Circle	138
33	The Future	140
34	Tools	142
35	About the Author	148

INTRODUCTION

I believe that it's important to highlight that I have no special skills. As you'll learn, I probably know less about computers, technology, web design, and programming than the average person. Odds are that I know less than you. My focus has consistently been on the internet and, eventually, search engine optimization. I just outsourced the rest.

You'll learn about how I struggled to create a successful business and made quite ridiculous mistakes. You'll also discover how I failed miserably, lost everything, and then had to win it all back. You'll learn how my most profitable ideas were the simplest. How I created a small four-figure income for months on end from less than five minutes of work.

You'll uncover how I found small loopholes in order to rank well in Google, only to have those loopholes plugged. This resulted in having to find a new secret recipe to receive Google love.

What's most important, and that I hope you'll take away, is the mindset. You don't have to settle with working a job that you detest. It is possible to earn a second income from the internet…or even make it your exclusive income to then quit your day job.

I made many mistakes and still managed to succeed. It's not because I am more intelligent than the average person nor is it because I have access to more tools. It's simply that I was more committed. I hope that you can learn from my mistakes and my achievements.

I also hope that you will gain a small nugget of wisdom, or perhaps a eureka moment: Something that will enable you to combine some of my experience with your own to generate incredible internet wealth.

I tried promoting my own products, but for me I had far more luck with affiliate programs. How you decide to go about your business will be up to you. Try not to shake your head at some of the early easily-avoidable errors I made. In my defense, I was nineteen years old when I started.

Also, some of the screenshots were used from the internet archive, which will explain any broken images that you see. Another important note is that many of the websites that are discussed are no longer operational.

Thank you for reading. May all of your dreams become realities.

WHAT IS AFFILIATE MARKETING?

Before continuing you should be aware of what affiliate marketing is. It's simply a way for a "merchant," which is a company with a product or service, to generate cost-effective marketing.

The merchant pays an "affiliate" a share of revenue or a fee for sending over visitors that purchase a product or service.

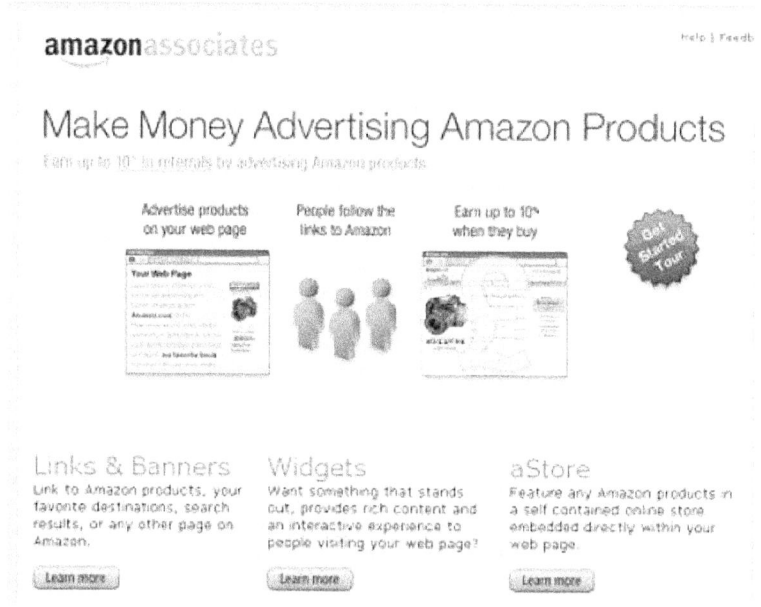

Almost every large on-line retailer has an "affiliate program." For instance, Amazon allows affiliates to sign up and send traffic from their own websites. This traffic is sent from a unique referral URL that tracks the affiliate responsible for a sale.

Commission size is dependent on the merchant as well as the type of product. It can range from 1 to 3% for electronics, all the way to 50% for dating or even 75% for e-books. At the end of this book, I will highlight which affiliate programs are the most profitable and which industries offer the highest returns.

THE BEGINNING

It was a cold winter day in 1999. To my relief, Walmart had just rejected my job application. My father had pressured me to apply but I had no desire to actually be employed at a Walmart. I was a high school dropout, trapped in Fort McMurray, the northernmost part of Alberta, Canada. My job prospects were nonexistent. The problem was that I was being pressured to work at an oil rig.

Oil is the big economy in Alberta, especially in that section of the province. Working in an isolated, cold community, with almost no women, was not what I wanted out of life. My options seemed limited. I had tried my hand at novel writing but, being nineteen, I lacked the life experience.

I had a purchased my first computer less than six months beforehand. Since owning it, I had accessed the internet to frequent Yahoo Chat Rooms, which were popular at the time. I had negligible computer experience, zero programming knowledge, and absolutely no experience with web design. I had no clue what html was, an FTP program, or any of the other things that comprised the internet.

What I did know was that the internet was revolutionary. It was flourishing, with newscasters raving about how it was going to transform the world. I figured the internet offered the best means of escape. I could create something out of nothing: my previous work experience, my lack of education, it all meant nothing. On the internet, everyone has an equal footing. A person could make something out of nothing and create unlimited wealth. It seemed like a no-brainer.

YAHOO AUCTIONS

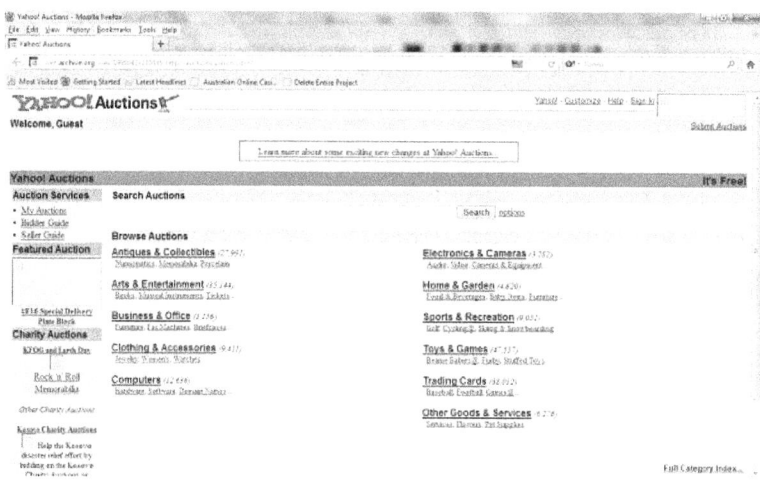

My first foray into earning money was accidental. I was browsing a Coles book store in a local mall. Coles was one of the largest book chains in Canada, and it was later acquired by Chapters to become the leader in Canada. (Comparable to Barnes and Noble in the USA.) As I was browsing the bookstore, I couldn't help but notice that the bargain bin had beautiful hardcovers selling for between $1 and $5. A light bulb went off in my head. It seemed logical; surely someone somewhere would find more value than $1 in these books. The books had cover prices of up to $40 and were on various topics, such as chess strategies and a biography of Stalin. I purchased $50 worth of books and returned home.

That night I listed all of the books on Yahoo Auctions. At the time, the auction service was free and significantly less competitive. I listed the books at the same price that I had paid for them, with a reserve set to $9.95 with buyer paying shipping. Before I knew it, the books were being bid on. The return on investment was anywhere from 1000 to 2000%. In theory, the return was high, but this involved a lot of work.

This technique of earning money was limited and faced several obstacles. The first problem was Canada's being a smaller market, with few Americans wishing to purchase books from north of the border. This limited my audience exponentially.

The second problem I had is that this was before PayPal or e-payments were invented. Buyers were sending checks via snail mail and it could take three weeks or more to receive a check. After all, who would pay express delivery for a $15 book? Unfortunately, sometimes I would deposit a check and it would bounce after I had shipped the book. I did not want to have buyers waiting a month for a book to be shipped and it took exactly a month for a check to clear. I tried stating that I only wanted money orders, but half the time, it was still checks that were received.

The third problem was that my inventory was low. Coles only had several books that were discounted, and the last thing I wanted was to buy 10 copies of the exact same Stalin biography. These were books that were desired by a select few, but they were not exactly best sellers.

Even without these problems, Yahoo Auctions was very time intensive and it encountered the time conundrum. It was no better than working a regular job. By the time I factored in writing the description in the auction, communicating with buyers, depositing checks, and driving to the post office to mail the books, it was too labor intensive for too little profit. In essence, I had created a job for myself. The last thing I wanted was a job.

A job to me represented the worse possible way of earning money. It takes people years to realize this and sometimes people never realize it. With a job, you are tied to working one hour for one hour's income. This is unproductive and cannot possibly be scaled upward. I am not sure why this was so obvious to me, even at nineteen, when all my friends were happy with earning $20 an hour working at an oil rig.

At $20 an hour, even if I worked 12 hours a day, it meant that the most I could earn in a month was $7200. That was assuming I worked every day for 12 hours a day. Factor in Canadian taxes and that would leave less than $5000. A goodly sum, but not exactly life changing. Also facing reality, there was no way I could or would work that much. A more realistic paycheck at a good paying job would be $5000 with $3000 left after taxes.

So why in the hell would I want to do something as silly as getting a job? Or continue with Yahoo Auctions, which was too limited in scope?

In essence, I gave up on the auctions model of earning income. After I had given up and eBay became huge, more and more people jumped on the auctions bandwagon, which just drove margins down. A person could earn a living by creating a job for themselves, but unless you had your own product you could not exactly get rich from it. I moved on.

ALL ADVANTAGE

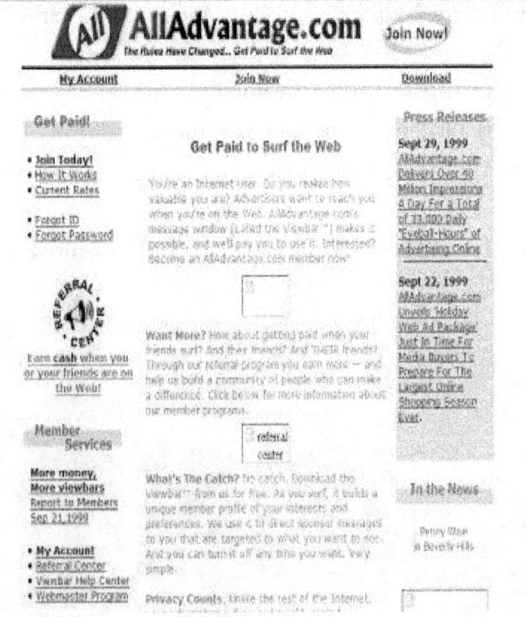

One day, while scouting the chat rooms, I heard of this amazing new technology company that was taking the internet by storm. The name of this company was AllAdvantage. They were paying members up to $20 a month to surf the web while looking at a rotating advertisement that would take up a third of your monitor. While $20 a month was not life-changing money, it was quite shocking to see what people would do for this type of income. You'd have people surfing the internet all day while having to look at these dumb ads to earn that extra $20.

I researched AllAdvantage and quickly stumbled upon the affiliate program that they owned. It was the first time I'd heard of the term affiliate program, I read up on it and was shocked. Here was a company that would pay me a commission every time someone else I referred to the program earned income.

Why would I worry about earning my own $20 a month when I could earn a share of what everyone else was earning? This was a lightning bolt of insight. It focused me more on the power of what the internet could accomplish. I searched "get paid to surf" and "all advantage," as well as other terms that were specific to this new product.

What I stumbled upon was forum posts, and a mad rush amongst the AllAdvantage members to share this new product with the internet community. Every deadbeat was pretty much trying to earn the $20.

It then dawned on me that I could create a website and get listed in the search engines for people who searched "get paid to surf." This certainly was better than what other members were doing, which was e-mailing friends and spamming forums.

I had no experience with web design or web hosting. I was low on funds so I tried doing things on the cheap. I signed up with Freeservers, which offered me free web hosting. The domain I would use would therefore be http://mysitename.freeservers.com. It was a pretty horrid way of doing business, but I didn't know better. The internet was in its infancy and the internet back then did not contain the same level of information as it does now. In this day and age, the internet offers so much data on how to earn money and other pertinent information that was simply unavailable in the dinosaur age of 1999.

So I created a banner farm on the Freeservers web host. I posted a banner for AllAdvantage. I also had located a handful of other new "get paid to surf" programs and quickly listed them all. Basically, the banner farm consisted of nothing but 468x60 banners with a small description under each banner. Oddly enough, I would use this technique of building a website for quite some time as it worked well.

Internet gurus claim that banners do not work. What they fail to mention is that banners do not work if the traffic is not targeted. If the traffic is targeted, and someone is searching out a product and the banner can satisfy that need, banners work well.

This was especially true in the year 1999. The beauty of a banner is that it's simple for newbies as it only entails copy and pasting html codes. There is nothing wrong with using banners. If someone is searching "get paid to surf" and you offer banners of companies that offer this service on your website, the conversion will be high.

Before I knew it, I had hundreds of consumers in my downline, with the bulk of them surfing the internet with ugly adverts taking up half their monitor. What some people were doing was running simultaneous "get paid to surf" programs. It was quite ridiculous and a bit shocking that people would resort to this to earn next to nothing.

I started earning hundreds of dollars every month, but then advertisers who were on these "get paid to surf" networks realized something. The advertising was worthless; they were throwing money out the window. The advertising was not targeted, and after all, what were you going to advertise to someone who clearly had no money if they resorted to watching ads full-time for the equivalent of $0.75 a day?

Advertisers dumped these programs in droves. Soon the programs were offering earnings of up to $5 a month to watch full-time ads, and that was too little incentive even for the hardcore enthusiastic surfer. The advertisers dried up, and the "get paid to surf" revolution was over with as soon as it began…and, of course, my earnings dried up to nothing.

I was back at square one but I had learned two words that would change my life. Those words were "affiliate marketing."

MY LAST REGULAR JOB

I was under pressure to apply at the oil fields. I was under even greater pressure to give up this nonsense idea of making a living from the internet. After all, the internet was a fad, and no one understood how it was possible to earn anything from this fad. Even if I pointed out the net worth of companies like Amazon, eBay or Yahoo, people ignored the data. They dismissed the earnings as flukes, or else they just disregarded the information, as it was contrary to their core belief.

Even today people have a difficult time accepting the fact that a person can make a completely acceptable living off the internet. These are the same people who will spend an hour every day on Facebook, buy books on Amazon, and order electronics from Overstock.com.

The year prior to this, my father had purchased a minivan along with a used $2500 steam-cleaning machine. He had attempted to earn a living by running a carpet-cleaning business. He'd given up quickly, as the oil field offered a more reliable and consistent income. I turned to this machine in an attempt to make temporary cash until the internet business was successful.

I created a flyer and mailed it to every single household in the city. This created an average of 2 to 3 jobs a day. The job consisted of visiting someone's home and cleaning the upholstery or carpet. In-between these jobs, I was focused on affiliate marketing.

I created a bunch of websites on Freeservers and other free web-hosts. My friends watched me waste all this time on the internet and were disappointed that I refused to go out and drink or get high, which was their favorite recreational activity.

I would have people dropping by at every hour of the day, wanting to get stoned. The clue that I had to escape the hood was when my neighbor dropped by at 3 a.m. I heard urgent knocking on the door. I dragged my butt out of bed and was greeted by my smiling neighbor. He was distraught. He'd spent all of his drug money and, in an effort to get high, he wanted to use the household chemicals I had stored underneath the sink.

Watching my neighbor sniff WD-40 with his best buddy was a stark reminder that I had to get the ball rolling. My neighbor left, and this became a routine with him: visiting every week to see what new chemical cocktails I had. I never mentioned all the cleaning supplies that were in the minivan; it was difficult enough coping with watching someone destroy their body like this. I didn't want my neighbor bashing the door in if I refused him entry, but I also didn't want to see him pass out.

One month rolled by and all of a sudden I had a check in the mail. The check was for $0.80. I remember thinking that the postage cost more than the check amount. I never cashed the check, for obvious reasons, but I wish I had kept the check so that I could have framed it. This was my first income from a true affiliate business (AllAdvantage was more of an MLM scheme).

The majority of people would have been discouraged at such a tiny income. I was overjoyed and enthusiastic for the future. This symbolized that it was possible to earn money by creating websites. The $0.80 reflected my having signed up a customer.

I was a lot more focused than before. A second month went by, with me ignoring the neighborhood degenerates and focusing on the carpet cleaning business for short-term income and on the internet business for long-term income. At the end of this second month, I received a much larger check: $8.00.

My income had shot up more than 1000%. If I could earn $8, all it meant was that 10 times more people had to find my website to earn $80, or 100 times more people to earn $800, or 1000 times more people to earn $8000.

At the time, I was using free software to create banner farms. The software was not very functional. I went to a local computer store and found a Microsoft program called FrontPage 2000. I purchased this for $200. I could now create better looking banner farms. The funny thing is that from that day forward until now, I have relied on FrontPage 2000. This outdated software was simple and intuitive to use, and it was exactly what I needed. It allowed anyone with no programming experience to create simple websites.

So another month rolled by. I was creating glorified banner farms and I would exchange homepage links with websites of similar quality. I would also submit my websites to popular web directories.

At that time I had no clue what search engine optimization was. Search engines were a lot more basic: they would locate your website based on the keywords in your content. Here I was getting traffic from AltaVista, Yahoo, HotBot, and Dogpile, as well as dozens of other long-forgotten search engines.

A third month went by and all of a sudden I received a handful of checks in the mail. One check was for $600; the other checks were smaller but together they amounted to a few thousand dollars in earnings.

I never bothered mailing out more flyers for the carpet-cleaning business. A couple of odd calls still came in, so I would head out every few days to clean someone's house, but that was it. Cleaning carpets was effective for short-term income, but the machine I had wasn't very efficient, which meant I had to work three times harder than if I had a state-of-the-art cleaner...and at the end of the day it had been a short-term solution for a short-term problem.

I kept diligently working on the internet business. By this time, I had a $500 credit card, which meant I could spend real money on the business. I bought some .com domain extensions and gave up on using free web-hosts. For people outside of Canada, this might come as a surprise that Canadian banks are so backwards...but Canadian debit cards are not tied to Visa or Mastercard.

This meant that I could not use a debit card to spend money on-line. Canadian debit cards were basically good for spending money in Canadian stores or at ATMs. Finally, by getting approved for this $500 credit card—from Walmart, of all places—I now had access to spending money on-line. All of a sudden, I could advertise, buy web hosting, etc.

I stayed in place, living with my father, for that fourth month. This is when, all of a sudden, my friends were realizing that this was not a fad. Real income could be generated. While they were slaving away in -40 degree weather, I was working from the comfort of home. After another month of earnings, I was now up to over $5000 in income per month.

The money was huge to me at the time, but it was nothing compared to what would come next. I decided to relocate to a different city. I needed to get away from the drunks and druggies that I associated with. I wanted nothing to do with them.

I drove seven hours south to a city that was more accessible to the rest of the world. It wasn't a great location, and it was still as cold as hell, but it offered me an escape from the crazies that would visit my apartment to access my household chemical supply. Unfortunately, I had no employment references and no rental references that a landlord could call. This forced me to settle for the only landlord that would take me in. Rent was $525 a month for a ghetto four-plex. But I was happy. I would be living on my own, and so I moved in.

THE REAL MONEY

The New Year rolled by, with a new millennium starting, and I was now in the fantastically boring city of Red Deer, Alberta. I was diligent in working on promoting affiliate programs. Checks were coming in via snail mail, and soon enough the UPS and FedEx delivery men knew me by name. I would be up working all night—sometimes until 5 a.m. Like clockwork, I would hear the doorbell ring at 9 or 10 a.m., which would snap me awake to rush to the door to pick up my latest FedEx.

I was meeting new people and sometimes they would peek behind my desk. I would get weird looks when they would pick up a check for $5000 from a foreign country, and I would simply remark that I had forgotten to cash that check. I was so disorganized that I would sometimes lose a check at the bottom of a drawer.

I knew I had made it when one morning I received a phone call from my bank. Half-asleep, I answered, and they wanted to confirm a foreign wire transfer for the amount of $35,000. I remember the precise amount; it was far more than any single check I had ever received. It was more money than a lot of people were earning in a year...and it was from promoting one affiliate program for the previous month. I acknowledged that I was expecting the wire and hung up.

I was in a daze. I was still not used to living large and, up until that point, I had put all my earnings into a savings account. I stayed home working from dawn until dusk. The only time I escaped from my cave was to go grocery shopping. I was so focused on work that spending money and living large didn't even pop up. I paid rent, bought groceries, and ordered a lot of pizza.

I was still driving the minivan, which was a piece of crap. One day, driving by a car dealership, I decided I needed a new car. I had received that huge wire transfer, so I would apply those funds toward a new vehicle.

I promised to pay cash, and I negotiated the price down, including sales tax, to precisely $35,000. This was my set limit and I would not spend $1 more. They agreed with the purchase price. I don't think they believed I would proceed with it, but I rushed to my bank and got a bank draft and returned within twenty minutes.

Purchasing a new car was an amazing feeling. I now had the freedom to pursue my dreams. All I had in my rotten four-plex was outdated furniture and a crappy desktop, but now I had a new car that reflected what I had achieved.

CRAZY NEW IDEAS

My affiliate websites were generating some pretty nice cash flow. I was clearing over $50,000 a month—not bad for having some really ugly websites! I had never learned to do web design and up until this point I was still throwing websites together that were pretty horrific looking.

It was also a time when I would test the market and see how far I could take being an affiliate. I tried dozens of new ideas every day, most of which failed, but sometimes I got lucky, really lucky.

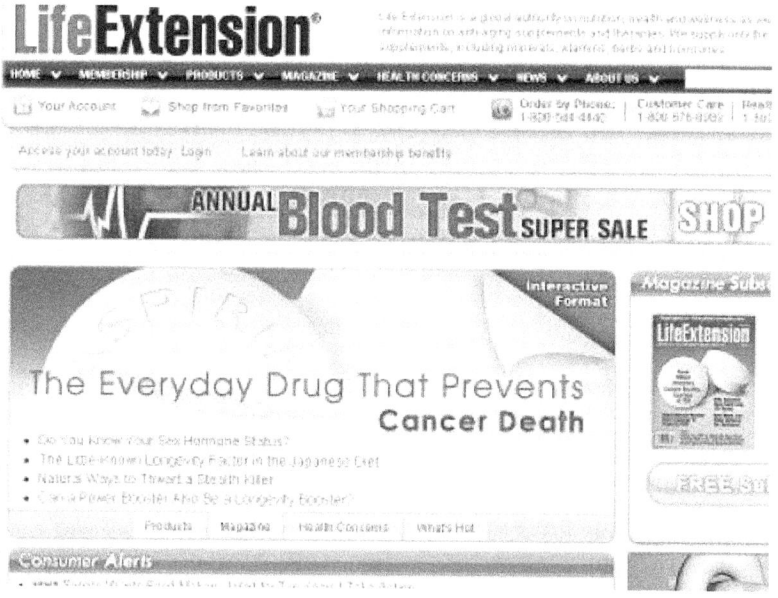

I was reading a lot about health and extending the human life span, which caused me to stumble upon the Life Extension Foundation. Of course, they had an affiliate program, which forced me to sign up. The problem was that I didn't have a health site. So what I did was search where the LEF was listed. I discovered that they were not listed on http://www.dmoz.org.

What is dmoz.org? It stands for "The Open Directory Project." At the time, it was a popular directory, as it was intended to be unbiased and to link to all of the best websites in the world. It was the answer to the cluttered and outdated Yahoo Directory. Dmoz was also run by volunteers.

I didn't want to create a website for the sole purpose of listing it at dmoz.org. I was lazy, so I simply signed up for a web-hosting account at a random URL and inserted my affiliate code in a frame. The URL was irrelevant; what I wanted was the IP address to open up with LEF in an invisible i-frame. To a visitor, it would look like they were visiting LEF. The only difference was that the URL they were visiting was an IP address, such as http://99.99.99.99

I submitted my IP address along with the relevant information concerning the Life Extension Foundation to the appropriate health category. After all, this website should rightfully be in the directory; the only difference was that I listed it with a different URL and with my affiliate code.

Less than a week later, I was listed in dmoz.org. I earned anywhere from $400 to $1000 a month for over a year, until the website was removed by a more knowledgeable editor.

All in all, it took me less than half an hour to set up an IP address and to submit the website. It was a huge return on my time…and my cost was $8 a month for the web hosting.

I was receiving the quarterly LEF newsletter for affiliates, and at one time, I was listed as a top-five affiliate. I am sure the other affiliates had legitimate websites and a more exhausting workload. It didn't matter; I was just looking for easy cash.

I spent some time searching Dmoz and trying to find other opportunities to list websites, but I never did find another opportunity. However, it did teach me that sometimes you just have to try. The highest return did not necessarily involve the most work or cost the most money.

Around this time, goto.com was becoming a significant player in the search industry. They were carrying out massive amounts of advertising and people were using the search site, as the results were quite relevant. GoTo later changed its name to overture.com, which was later acquired by Yahoo.

At the time, GoTo was a god-send for affiliates. No longer was I required to create websites and hope they would get picked up by the search engines. Yet less hope that I was listed high enough to receive traffic.

GoTo was a pay-per-click business model which, at the time, was quite innovative. They introduced it long before Google AdWords came along. I loved the flexibility of paying for traffic.

With a pay-per-click search engine, whoever paid the most would be listed the highest. For instance if you searched "car loan," first place might be paying $2.00 a click, second place $1.97, third place $1.80, and so on, until there were no advertisers. Once all the ad spots were taken up, the backfill was provided by Inktomi.

I was quite taken by the pay-per-click model. To me, it was a win–win situation for the search engine, the advertiser who could target consumers, and the consumer who could directly locate what he was searching for.

So I still used my $500 credit card, as I was unable to get another credit card because I had no legitimate work history and no verifiable income. Every day, I would basically deposit $500 and then top up the credit card, and the next day I would spend another $500 and so forth.

At first, I was only advertising my own websites, but that seemed very limiting. I could not possibly create a website for every topic known to humankind. After searching the results on GoTo, it became apparent that people were directly advertising affiliate links. So I then listed my affiliate links, directly advertising them under specific and relevant keywords. Sometimes I would spend more than I earned. When that happened, I reduced the bids or nixed the campaigns. Overall, I was earning more than I was spending.

Unfortunately, GoTo became so popular that bidding wars would ensue and, before you knew it, the margins became too tiny. I kept most of my listings up but refused to partake in unprofitable bidding wars. The result was that my affiliate links were listed but not high enough to generate huge traffic. I kept earning income but I gave up on spending too much time with GoTo, as I realized the prices would just continue to escalate.

I remember looking several months later and people were paying up to $40 a click for keywords from which I could not possibly earn a profit by paying more than $3 a click. GoTo was a golden business model that I would later try unsuccessfully to emulate.

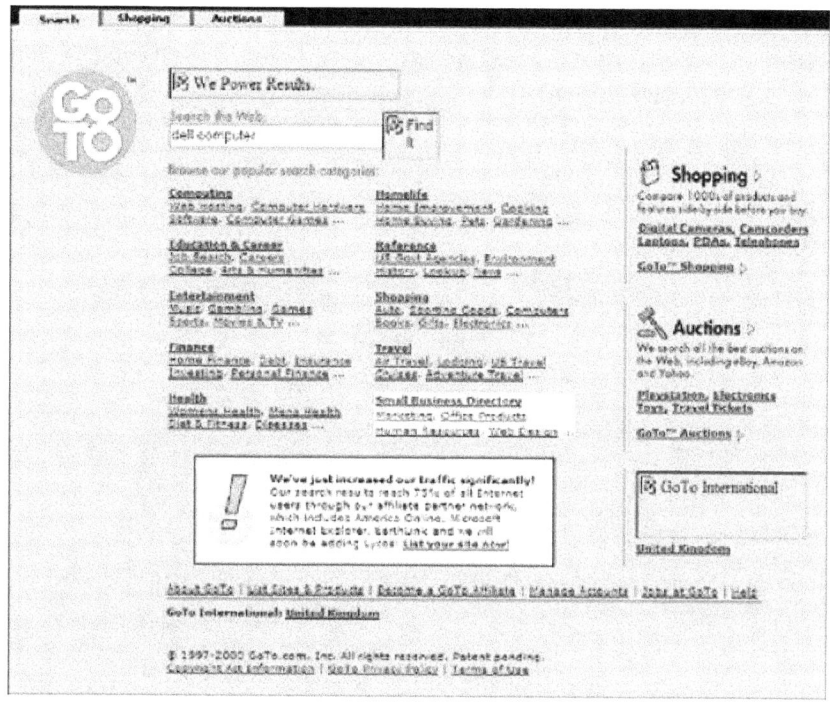

That being said, GoTo was not the only pay-per-click search engine. There were several new search engines that modeled themselves after GoTo and after AllAdvantage. They were a hybrid of both. These were the new "get paid to search."

SearchCactus was the most popular of these search engines. In essence, you could sign up as a member, and every time you searched, you would then see an advertiser listing. For example, if you searched for "shopping," you might see the first search result bidding $0.10. As a member, if you clicked on this listing you would earn $0.05.

SearchCactus became popular among a small niche. It basically had the same type of members who would frequent AllAdvantage. The problem for advertisers was obvious but that did not prevent advertisers from trying this new type of advertising. What it did cause was very low bids. The average price for a keyword was $0.02 (which was the minimum bid), and I wanted to capitalize on this.

What would users who want to get paid to search the internet be interested in? Anything shopping or involving spending money was not it. I then realized that sweepstakes were hugely popular. There was an affiliate network called OnResponse.com which was paying $0.70 every time a member signed up for a sweepstake. Clearly, these users were interested in trying to win free money or free products. I decided to make a sweepstakes website and I listed it in SearchCactus.

Before I knew it, the sweepstakes site was earning money from SearchCactus members. It was approximately $200 in monthly earnings with the limiting factor being that I could only promote the site under relevant search terms such as "sweepstakes" and "contests."

The main problem with sweepstakes was that the return was small so I had to do very cost effective marketing I had designed the website for SearchCactus but I decided to list the website in other free locations that had high volumes of visitors.

Dmoz was at the time, and still is, the most important directory on the web. The reason for this is that Google relies heavily on this directory to influence the search results. A webmaster listed in Dmoz could easily have a huge boost in search engine rankings. I submitted the sweepstakes site to Dmoz and kept looking.

This is when I remembered go.com. Who was go.com? They were a volunteer edited directory owned by Disney. It's quite simply amazing that Disney had the best domain name for a search engine and later converted it into a simple Disney portal. But at the time, anyone could sign up to become a volunteer. This is what I did.

I signed up to "volunteer" for the sweepstakes section of the directory. I listed three or four other sites and then slipped my sweepstakes site into the directory. Before I knew it, this go.com listing was netting me an average of $700 to $800 a month. It was not bad for a campaign that took me less than a day to set up and that included creating an ugly website.

Still, I knew that there was something more that I could do with SearchCactus. I logged into Commission Junction, which is the largest affiliate network in the world. At the time they allowed affiliate programs to pay affiliates on a per-click basis. (This function was later disabled due to affiliate fraud.)

I found a shopping mall website that paid $0.05 a click. I knew that my traffic would not convert well so I was very happy with getting paid this much. What I did next was to create my fastest and easiest income stream

I logged into Search Cactus and set-up an ad campaign. I created a listing for the shopping network and then set the pay per click cost to $0.02. I listed the shopping mall under every single relevant shopping keyword that I could conceive of such as clothe, electronics, jewelry, etc.

I launched the campaign and set my credit card to auto-load. In theory, every time a SearchCactus member searched, he would see the listing for $0.02. He would click on the ad and earn a penny for himself, SearchCactus would earn the other penny, and I would earn a nice 3 cents profit.

I set the campaign and before I knew it I had earned $2000+ profit my first month. I then increased the number of keywords I was bidding on and earned even more after that. The ironic thing is that I was concerned that the traffic would be garbage and that the affiliate program would terminate my relationship. I feared they would refuse to pay the money I had earned.

As far as the affiliate program was concerned, this was legitimate traffic. Most people were trying to cheat pay-per-click affiliate programs by sending fake bogus traffic. To my surprise, I received an e-mail stating they would increase my payout to $0.07 a click! My income went up quite significantly I was suddenly earning $0.05 profit per click. After maximizing all the traffic that I could send, I was netting over $5000 profit a month.

This money with SearchCactus was the easiest money I have ever earned. This taught me something valuable. The simplest ideas, the ones that are the easiest to pull off, can sometimes become the most profitable. If anyone claims that something is too easy, that it can't possibly work or else everyone would be doing it, that person might possibly be right—or else they could just be viewing things the wrong way.

When it comes to being successful anywhere, including the internet, it's all about mindset. Mindset is what I want to educate people about.

Of course, you can't replicate what I did, but what you can do is to learn about the strategies that I employed. It's important to learn that nothing is permanent. There will always be new opportunities and new ways of doing things. You just have to keep your eyes open for these opportunities.

Even Coca-Cola, the largest beverage company in the world, has to constantly evolve and reevaluate how they manage their business. Market leading technology companies such as Google and Apple are always reinventing the wheel.

When you see an opportunity, you can't think twice. You have to reach out and grab hold of that opportunity and claim it as your own. Otherwise, life becomes full of regrets, full of what-ifs. Of course, what you try might not work, but then try again; no one is holding you back but yourself.

Did I believe that I could earn $5000 a month by creating a search campaign that would take me less than 5 minutes to set up? Of course not—not in my wildest dreams. It was a far-fetched idea, but no one else was doing it, so I had nothing to lose by trying.

What is important is not having someone explaining a money making formula that works. If there were a magic formula and it were widely known, everyone would use it until profit margins became insignificant. For example, starting a business on eBay has long been one of the advertised winning strategies for riches on the internet.

Yes, you can get rich selling stuff on eBay, but unless you create a system that is unique to you, getting rich will be impossible. If you sell the same products as everyone else, you'd better hope that you can get these products at wholesale prices; otherwise, you can't compete. It's why I laugh when I see the same wholesale networks being advertised. Guess what? If 10,000 sellers have access to the same products with the same wholesale prices, that only means that profit margins have to plummet. The only way you can compete is by offering lower prices, free shipping, better customer support—things that in the end reduce your profit until it's barely enough to survive. Basically, it's a job that doesn't scale.

If you see a book or a late-night television infomercial that is advertising a get-rich-quick scheme go to bed or burn the book (well maybe recycle it). There is no winning formula that a guru will teach you for three easy payments of $24.99. There is no book that can teach you exactly how to make a million dollars over the internet. You have to use your unique perspective on the world and find the opportunity that is exclusive to you.

Opportunities are based on your life experience, on your knowledge. The winning formula is yourself. Read as much as you can, on a wide range of topics, experience life, travel, etc. Ideas come when they are least expected, but you have to be open to receiving them.

It's like those real estate books that claim to teach people how to purchase real estate with no money down. If it were that easy, don't you think the writer of the book would claim 10,000 of these houses for his own? Why would he share this secret?

Those writers get rich by teaching you information that is impossible to capitalize on. Those writers did not get rich from buying real estate with no money down.

Of course, this is not always the case. A book by Richard Branson provides an insightful lesson in how to grow your business. Then again, Richard does not claim to teach you how to make millions over night. He is not getting rich from his books; he is rich from his business.

Later, I will offer strategies and insights that can be applied toward your internet business. What I won't do is to claim that these ideas can make you rich. If you combine them with something that is unique to you and the way that you view the world, then, and only then, it might be a winning formula.

That being said, I had tried hundreds of different strategies. SearchCactus was the most effective one that involved the least amount of effort. The bulk of my income was still earned from traditional affiliate programs. Nonetheless, I was obsessed with pay-per-click search engines. I became greedy. I wanted my own GoTo.

CHARITY

Every month I would donate to humanitarian organizations, such as Doctors Without Borders. Being concerned about wildlife and the environment, I also donated to wildlife organizations such as the Dian Fossey Gorilla Fund. I strongly believe that being able to give back is one of the most rewarding things in life.

At this time, I also became intimately familiar with websites that were nonprofit, with the intention of raising funds for various causes. These were websites such as http://www.thehungersite.com and the http://www.therainforestsite.com . There were a handful of these popular organizations that revolved around a simple but effective concept.

Every day, a person could visit The Hunger Site and click on the "feed a child" button. After clicking on this link, a person would see various adverts. The money that advertisers spent would then go to the respective charity. This amounted to a few cents per visitor, but with hundreds of thousands of visitors, the donations did add up.

Greater Good, the network that *The Hunger Site* belongs to as of 2012, has donated over 26 million dollars to charity—an incredible sum for a nonprofit entity. If you are interested in raising profits for charity with no cost to yourself, I will provide a list of these websites in the *Tools* section.

HOW I MADE $10 MILLION FROM INTERNET AFFILIATE MARKETING

I fully respected these websites, but I also had an idea. Since there was a "get paid to search" pay-per-click search engine, why not a "search and donate" option?

My theory was simple. I would advertise the search engine at The Hunger Site and The Rainforest Site, as well as other charitable websites. My advertising funds would go to the respective charities directly.

Afterwards, the people who viewed my ad would be enthralled with the idea of being able to donate more money to charity for free. The only difference was that my search engine would offer relevant targeted ads. Unlike the get-paid-to-search group, this demographic was middle and upper class. Why wouldn't someone bookmark a search engine if they knew that half the profits went to charity?

To this day, I still believe this could have been a powerful tool for charity. Google earns billions every quarter. Can you imagine if they donated a percentage of this? This would be especially powerful if searchers had a choice of who they could donate to. The user experience would be exactly the same but the end result would be a lot of giving.

The problem was that I did not have the software for a search engine. At the time, over the shelf software was not readily available (how things would have been different if they had been).

And so I sought to hire a local programmer to build search engine software for me. That was the beginning of what ended up to be an avalanche of mistakes.

OBSESSED

To state that, at this point in time, I was not obsessed with the internet business would be a serious understatement. I would sometimes work for 20 to 24 hours straight and crash for 12 to 15 hours. I was waking up at all times of the day.

At one point, I ordered pizza 27 days in a row. I would order pizza at night and eat left-overs in the morning. Once in a while I would cross the street and buy myself jugs of V8 juice in a vain effort to get some type of nutrition in my body.

Other than going to the convenience store, the only time I would leave my apartment would be to network with my newly hired programmer. He worked from home but I was already getting frustrated. Things would take much longer than anticipated. The progress was slow. Then again, he was one person duplicating the same type of software that other companies used 100s of full-time staffers to develop.

While the software was being built, I kept working on churning out new affiliate sites. The process was quite simple. I would churn out a site and then try to write relevant content on that topic. I would really try to make it a destination worth visiting.

Later on, Google wrecked that business model when they became hugely popular. Prior to Google, a webmaster could effectively create a website and not worry about search engine optimization. I miss those days when content was king. The funny thing with the internet progressing is that content became less and less important. It's the opposite of the fallacy that Google sells to the public.

So at this point in time, I did not worry about SEO (search engine optimization). I just worried about creating content-rich websites and exchanging homepage links with similar websites. This worked wonderfully.

I made a game out of my earnings. Monthly newsletters from affiliate programs would feature the top 10 affiliates along with the number of leads they sent or the amount they earned. I would then lean toward pushing a specific program in an effort to make the list. It was a competition I created with myself. I would then see if I could become a top-three affiliate. Often times, they showed the rankings of the affiliates without the earnings, which would make me speculate on how much they were earning and I would then attempt to beat them.

After all this effort, I was hitting between $50,000 and $80,000 a month. Not too bad for a high school dropout. My rent was $525 a month; my monthly expenses combined were less than $1500 (I didn't go out). I would donate a significant amount to charity, but besides that, I was banking it all.

Around this time, I made the decision that I would retire by the time I was 25. It was ridiculously ambitious, but had I not screwed up so many times in the next two years, it could have become reality. But to retire at that age, I would have to get big fast. This meant that I would have to invest my affiliate income in other businesses. That decision would end up backfiring in many ways.

OMEGA SEX?

I was probably the whitest person in the city—which is saying a lot for somewhere that is brutally cold 9 months a year. Before you knew it, I had started hanging out with someone who seemed to have a different skill set. This person could design webpages, had some coding experience, and in theory could help out with my expansion plans.

I concluded that I could not launch the search engine by myself. I was already overwhelmed and overworked from trying to expand my affiliate empire. I wanted to get big quickly, but I needed assistance.

I agreed to set up a corporation for the search engine without researching it diligently enough. To keep things separate, the affiliate revenue would continue to go to my personal name. I was young, naïve, and did something that I would never recommend that anyone does. I went into business with someone I barely knew.

That night, with my new business partner John, we tried brain-storming corporation names. Every good name the .com extension was taken. We were playing around with different words when somehow the term "Omega" came up. Before I knew it, he wanted to add the letters FX at the end of Omega, as the domain name would then be available.

I was a bit stupefied by how irrelevant the name OmegaFX was. It made no sense; it sounded like some lame special-effects company, which was entirely different than what I envisioned. Regardless, I just wanted to move on and the company name was unimportant. After all, the company name would not be used anywhere. And so OmegaFX Marketing Group Inc became born.

When someone would phone the office, it always sounded like we were picking up the phone and answering with Omega Sex. I hated the name from day one and learned to really despise the name by the time the company was discontinued.

So here, being naive in the way the business world works, I walked into the local registries office with my new "business partner" and set up a corporation. We scanned the paperwork and I watched him fill in the blanks. When it came to the fields for number of shareholders, he wrote both our names. For the number of shares to each, he wrote 1.

A voice in the back of my head told me not to sign the document—that at a minimum, I should keep 51% of the shares as to have majority voting rights. After all, this deadbeat was offering next to nothing. It was my idea, and I was funding 100% of it. Hell, I would even have to pay him a wage.

I ignored the voice as being paranoid. Next thing you know, I had signed on the dotted lines. It was to be the worst financial mistake in my life, a mistake that in some form or another would end up haunting me for the next five years. A simple two-minute miscalculation, a rush to get big fast, had me ignoring common sense.

If you learn anything from this, it should be that please, do not ignore your inner voice. That voice is your reasoning. If something feels wrong, it's better to disengage, nine times out of ten. Had I not signed on that dotted line, I could easily be worth three times my current worth. The amount of lost opportunity, lost income, and stress is simply immeasurable.

And never start a business with someone you barely know. For all of my internet wisdom, I was pretty naïve in the way of the world and of business.

GETTING BIG FAST

I was watching American businesses and the dotcom boom in its full effect. I was shocked at the money that was being thrown around. I would login to Yahoo Mail and see adverts for Webvan. To me, it was a mystery how any of these companies survived. Here Webvan was a grocery delivery service that catered to a handful of American cities, yet they were advertising to a Yahoo member that had a profile set to Canada? It would be like my advertising a Russian website to American residents. It really made no sense.

Nonetheless, I wished I could have been American. If I were, I would have moved to Silicon Valley, as the opportunities there were ludicrous. Since this was not an option, I knew I could not find investors to fund my business. I would have to do it on my own.

I kept all of the affiliate income in my personal name and deposited it into my personal bank account. I would then transfer the money to the corporation.

We set up a downtown office and I hired two additional programmers. This made three full-time programmers to work exclusively on the search engine. More employees were hired for different tasks.

I explored what was becoming popular on-line and tried to emulate some of these websites. Below are some of the multiple projects I launched under the OmegaFX brand.

VirtuAds:

This was a banner exchange network. For every 3 banners that a member would display on his website (no personal homepages allowed), the system would display 2 banners on another member's website. This was a free service, and the monetization was that I would receive 1 out of every 3 banner displays. This would enable me to advertise affiliate programs or, better yet, to sell advertising.

VirtuAds was a break-out success. Hundreds of members turned into thousands of members. However, the service did have some problems, which prevented it from expanding.

Every new member would have to be approved, but then some members would play bait-and-switch games. We would approve one website and they would insert the html code on a different website. Other scammers would build scripts to auto-refresh the banner exchange with spoofed (fake) IP addresses. This would give them fake banner impressions, which would result in their having free banner impressions on other websites.

It was next to impossible to keep up with all the fraud. But the VirtuAds system was expanding exponentially, nonetheless. We didn't have to do much advertising. I would simply have a VirtuAds banner on member websites for every third banner rotation. This caused the website to be unprofitable but allowed it to grow fast.

At the time, I did not care about generating income. I just wanted to enlarge the empire. After some time, competitors began to come along and they offered more targeted member services. For example, a health site would only appear on another health site. This was a much better service.

This, combined with poor fraud control on our end, caused our service to lose popularity. But to be honest, it was never a huge focus for OmegaFX. I had allowed the ball to be dropped on this project.

Years later, banner exchange networks died out almost completely. Luckily, I sold this on eBay before it completely died.

A Domain Registrar Reseller:

Knowing what I know now about business, there is no way I would have touched the domain name registrar business. It meant entering a business that allowed us no way to differentiate ourselves from competitors except by lowering prices.

We signed up for a reseller account with OpenSRS, a Canadian domain name registrar. They would offer us wholesale prices of $10 per domain name (that was cheap at the time) and we could then offer a higher price to the consumer.

This was pure ridiculousness. We had nothing to offer that another registrar company could not offer as well. In fact, we offered less. Other registrars could upsell hosting and other more advanced services. Or the reverse was in effect: hosting companies would upsell domain names.

With thousands of OpenSRS resellers and tens of thousands of domain name registrars, the only differentiating factor was price. But the lowest we could go was $10. I started the names at $19. Other OpenSRS resellers had names selling for $12. At $19, it meant a profit of $9, which was not really a profit since buyers of domain names required customer support that we lacked the volume to offer properly. The other companies were earning a whopping $2 profit on each name!

On top of this, the OpenSRS system was so clunky that I hated to use it for my own domain names. We kept this service up but never really pushed it. Somehow, without advertising, we would get the occasional sign-up. To this day, I do not know how customers found our registrar website. Regardless, it was more of a pain than it was worth. At one point I had a red-neck real-estate agent come marching into our office claiming we would not allow him access to his domain name.

Hours were wasted trying to find this real-estate agent's lost password. OpenSRS managed passwords, so we had to get them on the phone and have the password manually reset, as the real estate agent no longer had access to the e-mail address he'd signed up with. All this for a whopping $9 profit, which ended up costing far more since I was paying for staff to babysit the agent.

The lesson learned here is not to start a business unless you can offer something to differentiate yourself from the marketplace. The only differentiating factor we could compete with was price, which meant driving down profit margins until they became nonexistent. The marketplace was also too competitive; trying to advertise our domain registrar service would have been impossible and created a negative return. Our website was greatnics.net, and it was also too generic a name to possibly brand.

Scenic Greetings:

www.scenicgreetings.com was a fun site and a nice change of pace. It was a simple concept. A visitor could send a virtual greeting to a friend or family member. We had non-targeted advertising that never ended up in any sales, but the theory was that if the site became big enough, it could then be resold.

It was a great word-of-mouth site. People would send friends or family a scenic greeting and those people would in turn become members. We featured cards with beautiful pictures from all over the world. The most popular were the beach cards. Someone would choose a beach card and send it with the message "wishing you and I were here."

This was a nice stress-free website. I forget why, but we sold it eventually on eBay. Membership had grown stagnant; it was still unprofitable but not really costing us anything. I do remember that competition was popping up like crazy, which might have influenced the sale. Had we invested in the website, perhaps it might have gone somewhere, but probably not. Nonetheless, it has a soft spot in my heart, as I personally used the service to send friends greeting cards.

Magazine Wave:

I really wanted to move away from promoting other people's products and to create my own shopping site in order to have affiliates promoting my product. This was the answer. The plan was to have a general magazine store that offered magazine subscriptions at fair rates. To find our audience we would then develop an affiliate program and feature it through Commission Junction.

Magazine Wave featured state-of-the-art web design and was exactly what shoppers were searching for. I located a great designer to create some appealing banners. I had located a wholesale distributor. Unfortunately when that relationship went south due to the misinformation he was feeding us, I was unable to find another wholesaler. No one wanted to deal with a company that was outside of the United States. At the time, it really felt like being outside of the USA was impeding us. The merchant account company to accept credit cards was charging double the going rate. We were basically paying the same rate that high-risk merchants such as adult and gambling sites were paying.

I had functional software and a beautiful website that converted traffic into sales. Commission Junction offered the opportunity to recruit affiliates in an industry with huge demand. Unfortunately, because of my location, I would lose the distributor. I was disappointed, but after reviewing my options, I had no choice but to fold and move on.

Until this day, affiliate programs automatically reject me because of location. Many retailers have software programmed to only accept US affiliates. Dish Network is an example of a corporation that screwed me. At one point, I was sending them dozens of sales a month, but more importantly, I had a huge downline of thousands of sub-affiliates from which I earned 5% of what they earned. This was all lost when a moronic corporate executive made the illogical decision to terminate relationships with all non-US affiliates.

Anyone who is located in America has, by default, a huge advantage over the rest of the world when it comes to internet marketing. I've encountered many problems where companies refuse to allow me to promote them. Fortunately this is changing with time as American companies realize that there is a world outside of the US borders.

Personal Safety HQ:

My second attempt at having my own product was for personal defense gear. These products could never be shipped outside of United States borders, as they would be confiscated by customs. I had located a wholesaler and they offered stun guns, pepper spray, hidden cameras, and other equipment that served a paranoid society.

The problem with these products is that I could not get a bank or a merchant account to touch us with a ten foot pole. A beautiful website, a great shopping experience: it all meant nothing if we could not accept credit cards.

This was another moment in which I could have gotten this off the ground, if only I had been in the USA. But in life, you have to deal with the hands that you are dealt.

On a good note, I later sold this website on eBay. Years later, the buyer contacted me and informed me that they were happy with the purchase. They had done some search engine optimization and were making a full-time living from this website. I was quite happy to learn this. Reading a success story, especially one that you had influence in creating, is always a positive experience.

Cool Log:

Creating businesses on the web was becoming increasingly popular and there were many websites that capitalized on this by offering statistical and analytical tools to verify the incoming traffic to your virtual property.

One popular service that I even tried advertising on was called Hit Box. At the time, Hit Box was the most popular service (although http://www.statcounter.com soon replaced them). With Hit Box in an easy-to-access graphical format, you could view the countries of visitors, the referral URLs, the search terms that people used to locate your website, and much more in-depth information.

Witnessing firsthand the growth of this market, I wanted to offer my own version. Cool Log was released; unfortunately, I should have avoided releasing a product that offered customers no clear benefits. Hit Box was simply better.

The lesson here is that unless you can offer something unique, having a program that offers users no clear benefit and no reason to stick by you is a no-win situation. Several hundred webmasters tried our tool, but most abandoned us for Hit Box or other competing solutions that were superior.

On top of that, the name was just a bit on the lame side.

Pop Zoo:

Similar in functionality to Yahoo-owned Geocities.com, & Lycos-operated Homestead.com, Pop Zoo was offering users a free homepage service. This was all the rage at the time. Pop Zoo was a fun and short name. The branding potential was huge, but it was difficult to get the software working as well as I would have liked.

The programming staff I had was too busy with the search engines so I used an off-the-shelf software package that did not offer all of the services I would have wanted to offer. This was probably a good thing, as offering free hosting and free homepages is a very customer-service intensive business model. If you ask any webhost, the people that pay money for webhosting are far less annoying than the freebie hunters who expect to pay nothing but demand everything.

Casino Fuel:

The last non-search engine website that I released was casinofuel.com. How Casino Fuel worked was quite simple.

Earlier that year, casinotrade.com was launched and it had taken the on-line casino world by storm. Affiliates and on-line casinos would sign up for this service and place a line of html code on their website. Whenever someone visited a casino site, a window would pop up in the background with a different member in the network. Similar to the way that VirtuAds worked, for every three exit windows you fed into the system, you would receive two in return. Casino Trade would then sell the inventory.

On-line casinos were spending tens of thousands to advertise on Casino Trade. I quickly launched Casino Fuel within a week of realizing what was happening.

It only took several months to notice that people were getting fed up with Casino Trade. Casinos were realizing it was hurting conversions and alienating customers. When I saw this, I listed Casino Fuel for sale and sold it to an on-line casino. I signed an NDA so I cannot disclose what this sum was or to whom I sold it.

Several months afterwards, this casino terminated the Casino Fuel service. I had exited that industry just in time. I spent very little money on the product, even less time, and it provided a decent return. It was to be the only program in the OmegaFX arm that would achieve anything viable.

BURNOUT

All this was happening fast; all of these websites were created and launched within five months of starting OmegaFX. In the meantime, the search engine software was being diligently worked on.

Every day, I would venture into the office first thing in the morning, eat lunch at Subway across the street, continue work until the office hours were over, and then head on home, where I would plug away on my affiliate stuff until nightfall.

I eventually tired of this routine. Four months previously, I had begun dating a nice girl and we had just rented a new townhouse in a friendly middle-class neighborhood. I needed to relax a bit or else I would have gone crazy.

I announced that I would not be frequenting the office as much. What ended up happening is that I would still be working on OmegaFX projects, but from home. It was the profitable affiliate stuff that ended up taking the brunt of the time cut.

I just could not continue with the internet being the focus of my life 24/7. I still invested long hours, but I also tried to find a bit more balance. Unfortunately, finding that balance was a challenge.

I was still significantly vested in the company. Every month, all my affiliate income was redirected to OmegaFX. I paid myself an average of $3000 a month, which allowed me to live conservatively, while I offered endless shareholder loans.

Unfortunately, by not spending as much time in the office, I missed some obvious warning signs of an impending collapse.

SEARCH ENGINES

I had initially wanted a "search and donate" pay-per-click search engine. This was to become the main focus. At the time I experienced concerns that not every advertiser would be willing to use our website for fear of fraud. It was then that I decided we would launch three search engines.

Fast2find.com:

Fast2find.com was to be the search engine that imitated the SearchCactus model. This was most likely to be the least profitable engine for the same reason that the growth of Search Cactus was limited. Advertisers would be reluctant to advertise on a site that rewarded members. Nonetheless, it offered the easiest marketing tool. We could rely on viral marketing. The word-of-mouth would be huge among the freebie hunter crowd. In theory, this could serve as a flagship product to initially recruit advertisers.

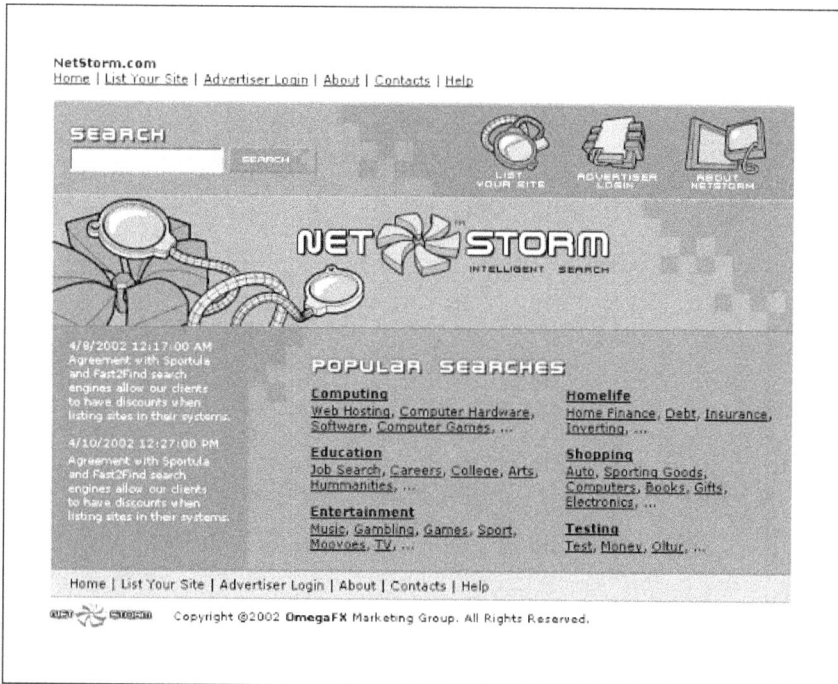

NetStorm:

I had seen the domain name for sale and quickly picked it up. Netstorm.com could have been a powerful brand. While the name was a little long, it was memorable. NetStorm would be our answer to GoTo. The main problem is that we had no idea how to get people to use our website. Even Google only became huge after a significant amount of free publicity on various news stations. Google won the lottery; I did not expect to get so lucky.

NetStorm never had the chance to fully develop. Above is a really ugly prototype that was a placeholder until a better design came up. I later sold the domain name, which I still regret to this day.

Sportula.com:

This was a temporary name until something better came around. Sportula basically means "to give"; unfortunately, the word" sport" could throw people off. Initially I had wanted to have visitors come directly to our website, but it later dawned on me that a better technique would be to partner with huge nonprofit or even ethical websites.

So these were to be the three search engines. I figured if the software was working on one, there was no reason it could not be duplicated two more times. Since I had launched the pay-per-click idea in order to generate profits for charity, Sportula was our test search engine.

EMPLOYEE INCOMPETENCE

Clearly, I was not in a good location for hiring staff. I should have relocated somewhere like Toronto or Vancouver. Instead, I imported employees, with one programmer moving in from Calgary (a city of 1 million plus) and another from British Columbia. The problem was that even with impressive resumes, the actual end delivery was disappointing.

The programmer with the best credentials (from Calgary) came into the office and he could not figure out diddly-squat. My head programmer eventually confided in me and instructed me that we had to lay the guy off. For the first two weeks, he had his head in programming books in an attempt to learn what we were undertaking.

At first it was assumed he was catching up on the different technology, but then it became clear he was going nowhere. This employee was released after a month. I felt horrible, as he had relocated. But in that month's time, he had written fewer than three lines of code. I could not seem to find anyone competent.

The head programmer who had first started the search technology was frustrating in his own way. He would show up at the office at all times of the day. We had a strict nonsmoking rule and he would be lighting up when I wasn't around. This was basically breaking labor laws. I must have reprimanded him a dozen times for this.

Unfortunately, we did find a really competent programmer near the end. This was a guy that lived for code. I knew when I first saw his car as he pulled in from British Columbia that this guy would be a wizard. He was driving a beater, and instead of buying a CD player, he had connected a computer with speakers that were powered by his cigarette lighter. He was listening to mp3 songs on his computer while driving. This is the ridiculous level of genius that you want to see in a programmer. This whiz was more productive than everyone else combined. It's too bad that he only worked for two months before everything collapsed.

THE SOFTWARE WONT WORK

Every time it seemed like we were approaching developing functional software, a new bug would be discovered. We then had to wait until the bugs were ironed out.

I was getting frustrated. I was redirecting all of my funds to OmegaFX and the corporation was earning next to nothing. In the meantime, my affiliate income was dropping as I could not focus on it. There was also a new search engine in town that was changing everything.

I mistakenly assumed that Google would be the best search engine around, and that being so advanced, doing anything to optimize my website would be frowned upon. I was under the impression that they would reward quality content. This was far from reality. Google needed to be optimized for, but I was too busy, so I was watching Google become a giant and I was ignoring my drop in traffic.

My income, which had been as high as $80,000 a month, was now in the $30,000 to $50,000 range. It sounds like a significant chunk but it really wasn't when you factored in employee and office costs. I gave myself a raise to a whopping $3500 a month, which did not leave me much once taxes were taken out.

The exception to this was when I was getting kicked out of my duplex. Management had discovered Oliver the cat, who seemed to enjoy sitting in the window. The problem was that this was not a pet-friendly complex. We were given an ultimatum: I had to relocate, or get rid of the cat.

Obviously, I was not going to get rid of my cat, since he was part of the family. I tried finding somewhere to rent but nothing decent was nearby. This was during the oil boom and accommodations were scarce. Our only option was buying a house or losing Oliver.

That month, I decided I would keep the income and not redirect it to OmegaFX. It was the only month I paid myself more than a nominal wage. All of the income was applied towards a down payment on a small home in the suburbs. It was pure luck that I decided to keep those funds for myself and to spend them on me. It was to be my only positive investment, which is ironic since it was the most basic of investments.

I just knew that things had to change. I knew all future income would have to be invested in OmegaFX or else the company would fold. I decided that we could wait no longer. We would do a soft launch of Sportula, even with the bugs.

FINDING ADVERTISERS

Releasing a search engine is a catch-22. No one is going to use your website if there are no search listings. You also can't afford to advertise to the public without advertisers. For search results, we bought the technology of a metasearch engine. This was essentially a copycat of Dogpile. Basically, we would have the results backfilled by various search engines and give credit for this. At a minimum, people would see something when they performed searches.

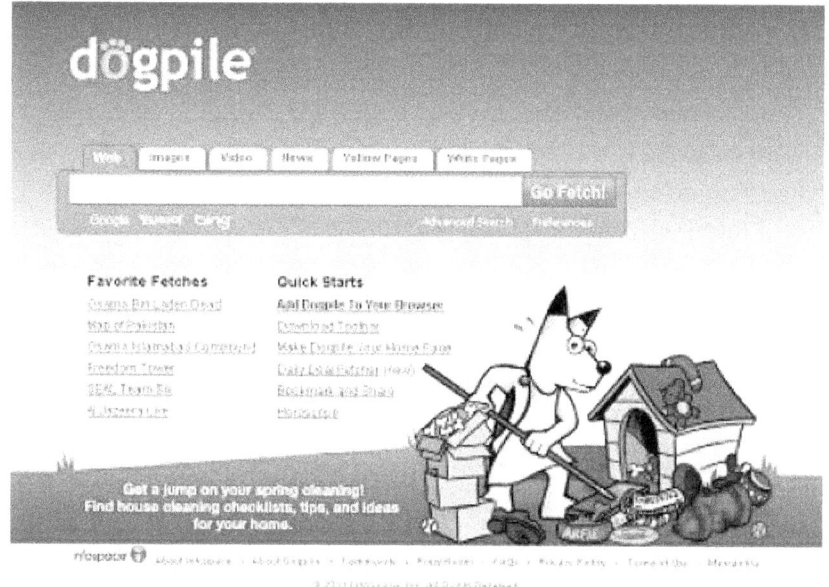

I knew that webmasters instinctively spied on each other's sites. I would often study where my competition was listed and advertising. I decided that my sites would have people spying on them. I listed most of my sites on Sportula, which also allowed to me beta-test the advertising interface.

I located problems, which, of course, forced more delays. But I eventually listed all my sites and I listed some major sites that I knew people would be spying on. The strategy was working; we started getting a handful of advertisers.

Regrettably, having advertisers with no traffic is inadequate. We had to find traffic and find it fast. I followed my initial idea, which was to advertise on sites such as The Hunger Site. The first campaign was actually on a similar site, but with the funds going to an ocean-related charity. This cost us $5000 and the resulting influx was a few thousand people visiting the website and then losing interest. Unfortunately, we were having server problems that week and the search engine results were frustratingly slow.

At the end of the day, the theory was proven sound. We could advertise in those locations, but the amount of income generated per visitor was next to nonexistent. We did not have advertisers for most of the terms people were searching for.

I then signed up for affiliate programs and listed different programs under specific search terms. I set the bids to $0.02 and while, in theory, this would cost me nothing, we were donating half of the click amount to charity, so it did cost us something. Unfortunately, I was one advertiser and could not list myself under every search term known to mankind.

Months went by and the software was improving but the results were still not up to my high standards. The programmers were quite simply incompetent. Around this time, sites to outsource webdesign and programming were becoming popular. A person could hire a company off of Elance or a similar outsourcing site and get quality work for cheap. I was considering doing this but was reluctant to lose all the progress we had achieved.

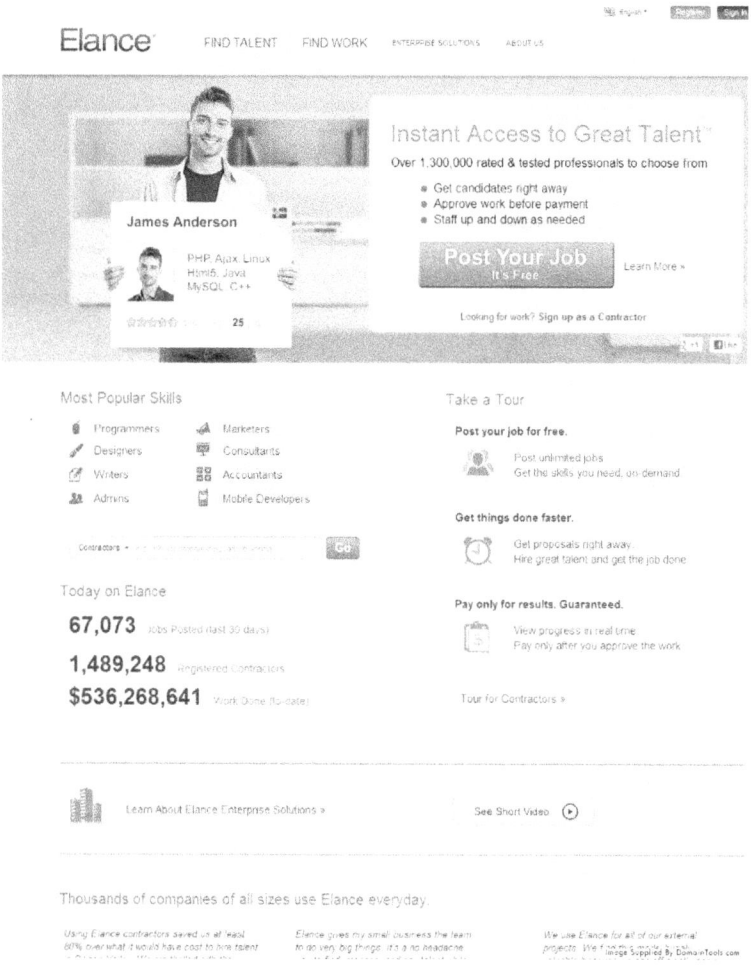

It's then that I gave the word to try and find partners for Sportula. We created a search bar that other websites could integrate. People could then search from Sportula, with visitors never having to leave the website they were on. We signed up a few partners but nothing major. Since 50% of the profits were automatically donated to charity, we'd have 25% to pay the partner and we would keep the rest.

It was then that we signed up a major network. At the time, care2.com had millions of devoted members who cared about saving the planet and all of its inhabitants. These were loyal web users who would spend countless hours filling out protest forms, visiting click-to-donate websites, and learning more about the environment.

We had the search tool on care2.com for a week. The amount of people using the search tool was so large that the server crashed. Had our software worked properly, this arrangement could have been intensely profitable, resulting in a successful business.

Just around the time our server crashed is when the wizard programmer from British Columbia arrived. He started rewriting all of the code. The software was starting to work properly. This whole time we just needed someone that even Google would have hired.

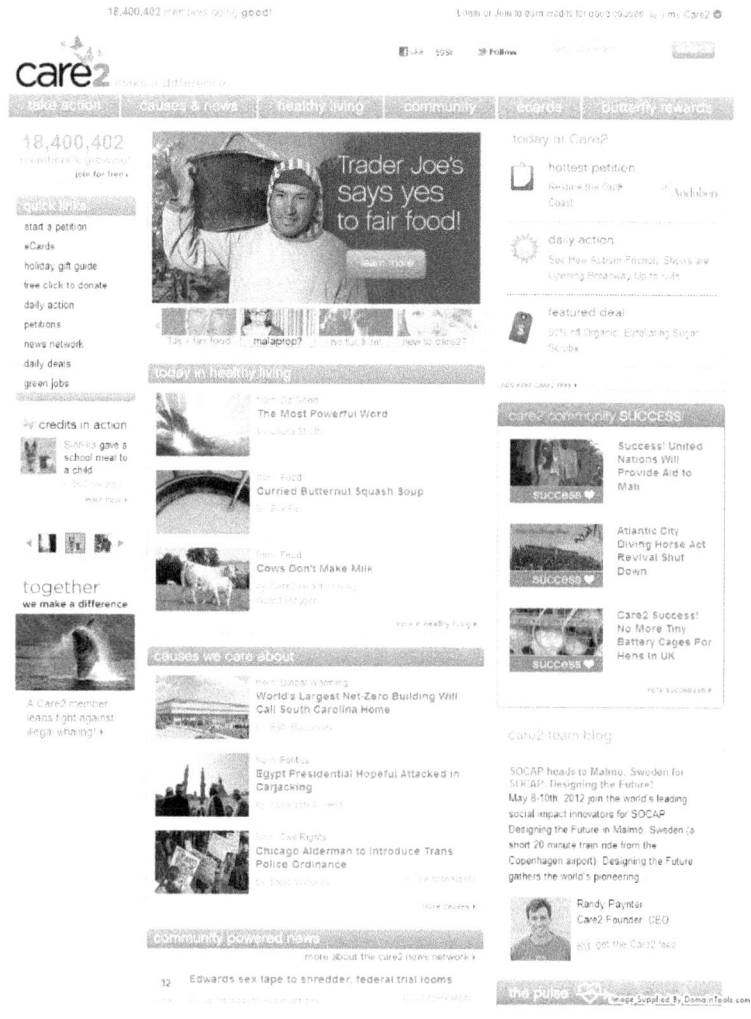

It was around this time; with losing care2.com as a partner, that I decided I needed a vacation. I announced my plans and before leaving was approached by John. Our lease was about to expire and our office location was getting annoying since it was impossible to find parking. On top of this, we were paying to be downtown for no logical reason.

John suggested that he would scout a new location while I was absent. I figured it was a good idea, as I was fed up with the location. In theory, a new location would be cheaper, and saving some funds was important. He showed me a prospective new location in the industrial area and I told him to investigate it.

I flew off to Nevada. When I returned, everything would be vastly different.

LAKE TAHOE

I was in Lake Tahoe when the decision was made that things needed to change. Even with the new programmer, it made no sense to continue operating OmegaFX as it was. The entire business was running from funds that I was investing. I knew that as soon as I pulled the plug, the company would essentially be dissolved. I didn't even care if OmegaFX continued; something had to change. I was considering keeping the wizard programmer on, and laying off most of the staff. They would be given enough notice to have a small window of opportunity to find alternative job arrangements.

I sent an e-mail about my ideas to John. I was adamant that we could find software on Elance or a similar outsourcing network. Bureaucratic red tape from having staff was cutting into our profits. Our head programmer was quite incompetent, and it was next to impossible to find proficient employees. I really wanted to minimize expenses and, most importantly, to increase profits.

After sending the e-mail, I completely forgot about work and proceeded to enjoy the Lake Tahoe area. I returned home earlier than anticipated and went to check my mail. Most affiliate payments were still expedited by check, so this was always exciting.

ANTOINE WALKER

When opened my mail, all hell broke loose.

LOCKED OUT

I opened my bank statement and a check was attached that I had apparently written. However, the signature was forged. It was a $5000 check made out to John's American Express card. I grabbed my cell phone and called him and said we have to talk. John mumbled something and hung up.

I jumped in the car and headed downtown. On my way to the office, I decided I should stop at the bank. Had I arrived five minutes earlier, or not phoned my business partner, I could have avoided a lot of grief.

As I ran into the bank, I saw him walking out with a bank draft in hand. I approached the bank teller and demanded to know what had just transpired. I learned he had just liquidated the bank account with a bank draft written to a corporate name that I was not familiar with.

I freaked out. The bank was supposed to require two signatures for any bank drafts or wire transfers. This is what happens when you deal with a Mickey Mouse bank. The teller had not noticed that two signatures were required.

I was pissed and raced off to confront my partner. He was, of course, gone. I then drove to our office.

It was completely emptied out. Our lease had not yet expired and I had not anticipated that we would relocate offices so soon.

I remembered the "new office" he had shown me prior to leaving. I drove there and I saw his car in the parking lot. I demanded entry into the office that held all of my belongings. A lot of my personal stuff was at the office. All of my personal paperwork for accounting and taxes was stored there.

They called the cops on me. The cops showed up and John showcased a document demonstrating the lease was under his name. They threatened to arrest me unless I vacated the property.

I had just returned home to my business account being liquidated. This account held most of my personal income, as it was to be used for future operating expenses. All of our office equipment and paperwork was no longer in my possession.

I called my girlfriend and explained what happened. We decided we needed a lawyer. I made an appointment for the following business day.

I returned home and logged onto my laptop. I wanted to secure my personal websites, as clearly, I was under siege. By the time I decided to do this, I realized that my most profitable websites that were generating 80% of my income were now under his personal name. He had transferred the domain names to himself while I had been on vacation.

I raced to save all of the other websites from being transferred and I quickly created new passwords for everything including my e-mail accounts. In the process of reviewing my e-mails, I found an e-mail from an affiliate program. The affiliate manager was asking if I approved of a payee name-change request.

I responded that I did not approve and requested more information. She forwarded me an e-mail that was sent from the secretary of OmegaFX. The e-mail was requesting that the payee name be changed from my personal name to a new corporation I had never heard of. I thanked the manager for her valuable contribution.

I have to give credit to the affiliate programs. The secretary had requested a payee name change to all affiliate programs I was signed up with and only one had agreed to the request. This program then changed the payee name back to my personal name.

I still had the affiliate programs paying me for old sign-ups. Other than that, I now had no money, no websites, and no documents. I had nothing.

JUSTICE?

At this point, I was stupefied, but still under the impression that, since there was obvious thievery, I could just rely on justice being served. I had never realized how useless the entire justice system was until that day.

After checking all of my e-mails, changing all of the passwords, and taking care of urgent business, I decided to visit the police. After all, I had a check with my name forged all over it. In most countries, theft over $5000 was a serious offense. The amount of the forged check was for this amount and that wasn't even taking into consideration everything else.

I sat down and filed a statement. I was then told that because I was in business with this person, it was my word against his, and they could not do anything. They advised me to get a lawyer. I tried explaining, in vain, that with everything else, yes, the corporation muddied the waters, but this was a check forged from my personal bank account to his personal credit card.

They would have nothing to do with it. As far as they were concerned, they would not get involved in any white collar dispute.

The police were of no assistance and were next to useless. I would have to sue.

The truth about the justice system in any country is that it's not about who is right or who is wrong. It's about who has the most money. The loser is the one who runs out of funds first. Only one problem: My enemy had access to all of my money.

I had next to nothing in my personal bank account. I was sitting at around $10,000. When paying a lawyer $250 an hour, that goes fast.

First things first. I was introduced to a process server. I drove him to John's condo, which was in a neighboring town. Luckily for me, I pulled into the parking lot just as he was preparing to drive away with his girlfriend. I blocked the obvious exit route.

The server got out of my car and handed over the paperwork. The look on my partner's face was priceless. He'd been served.

STARTING FROM SCRATCH

The reason I wanted to share this story is to prove that anyone can succeed on the internet. Clearly, this was a different era. It was now 2001. The internet is always evolving, and what had worked for me in the past was clearly not working anymore.

My most profitable websites were stolen. On top of that, my remaining websites were suffering huge drops in traffic. Google was now the king, and everyone had a love affair with this new search engine. I was still receiving traffic from Yahoo and MSN (later renamed Bing), but the traffic kept diminishing.

I had legal bills to pay. The justice system is slow, which in my case was both a blessing and a curse. Being slow meant I had time to raise funds. During the court process, many of the stolen sites were taken offline. I knew that being taken offline for extended periods of time was equivalent to website suicide. The search engines would delist the websites, and link partners would remove links I had taken months of my time to build.

At the end of the day, I wanted those websites back. There was no way I would allow my "business partner" to keep them, even for the sake of principles.

I was quite angry at how the employees were treated. With my partner now in control, the staff at OmegaFX was simply not paid. I preferred to give people a fair notice. Unfortunately, I could not afford to pay them.

I made the difficult decision to abandon the search engines I had worked on for the past year to just focus on earning income from affiliate programs. After all, lawyers had to be paid.

On top of this, the grease-ball argued that all of my sites belonged to OmegaFX. The judge was ancient and not internet savvy. He ordered all my websites to be placed in receivership.

So, while taking John to court, I lost access to my remaining websites. In essence, receivership meant my websites were dead.

My only advantage during the court process was that we were both burning through money fast. I knew John would run out of funds once the stolen money was exhausted. All I had to do was to create new websites and start earning cash so that I could fight him. It was clear that taking him to court was not about justice being served; it was about whoever could survive the longest by not running out of cash.

I had long ignored Google, thinking they would list the websites with the best content first. I had assumed they were more advanced than they really were. Google had always fed misinformation to the public and especially webmasters.

I could no longer create quality content and hope that search engines would appreciate it. I would have to learn SEO.

SEARCH ENGINE OPTIMIZATION

This is the most important aspect of running an internet business. In theory, websites are ranked in search engines according to quality. But this is a pretty ridiculous notion. How do you judge quality? What happens if there are 10 websites of identical quality, with great bloggers, who are consistently releasing fresh articles?

Google would have you believe that the best content shows up first. Computers do not know what content is considered best. They rely on an algorithm that, to this day, has changed very little.

For instance, you look up "news" in Google. Google could list small, locally based news sites, so what makes it decide to list larger news sites versus the small news station down the street? It looks at how many sites are linking to different news sites with the anchor text (linking title) "news" in it.

Odds are that the top 10 results will include Google News, CNN, BBC, Fox News, Yahoo News, and ABC News. For the sake of argument, we could have CNN ranking first under the search term "news." This would be because CNN has 100,000 websites linking to it with the term "news." BBC might have 90,000 websites linking to it with the term "news." BBC would then be second. Fox News could have 80,000 websites, which would then make it third.

That is the simplest way of explaining SEO. He who has the most links, wins. Of course, there are many other variables, so this is to keep the example simple. For instance, not all links are considered equal. One link from CNN or the homepage of Yahoo will be worth more than 1000 links from small unknown mom-and-pop sites.

So I had to learn how to perform SEO. That first month while the court proceeding were taking place, I frequented all of the SEO forums and tried to absorb as much information as possible. There were two clear problems.

The forums were full of misinformation and most of it was speculation. No one knew exactly what was working. There were the Google worshippers who claimed that content was king and that doing anything to manipulate your search engine ranking was bad. At the opposite end of the spectrum, there were black hat website owners who were speculating on how to manipulate the results in every way possible.

The information on the forums was inconsistent, unreliable, and, quite honestly, useless. After a month of scouting the forums, I quickly gave up. I did not have the time to figure out the optimal number of characters to be used in metatags, or guess how many words the optimal page should have. The only consistent characteristic that was described was that, in some form or another, Google loved links.

I decided that link exchanges were quite simply the best way of generating links quickly. Exchanging homepage links is what I previously had done, but anything more than a couple of links on your home page looked spammy. I was also afraid it could get a website banned.

And so I created interior pages devoted to links. These interior pages were linked from my homepage, and they would feature nothing but link exchanges. I tried doing the link exchanges myself initially, but it was clearly too time-consuming. I needed to focus on building more websites.

I then created a process:

1. I would hire a web designer on an outsourcing service, such as Elance.

2. I would insert the content, baners, etc, myself

3. I hired a company to build, maintain link pages, and find link partners.

4. repeat the above.

That was my whole process. As simple as ABC. I had learned early on that to earn significant income you need to keep things simple so that the process can be scaled.

At first, I owned only three websites and I waited patiently for links to be built. The results were almost instantaneous. The more links, the higher up in Google my website would appear under the specific search term I was targeting.

My income was still nowhere near what it used to be, but luckily for me, I started receiving affiliate checks right on time before my bank balance hit zero. I even had to stall the law firm for a few days until enough money came in to pay them an additional retainer.

I knew I had to invest, even with my funds dangerously low. I ordered the company that was building links to have three full-time staff working exclusively for me. These people did nothing but scout the internet for link exchange partners.

Finding link partners was a slow process, so I wanted to maximize the potential for growth. I decided that once partners were found for one website, we would just contact those webmasters repeatedly to exchange links with my new websites. Most webmasters were happy with this arrangement. Once they exchanged links with one website, they knew they could trust me with the new sites I would launch.

Several months went by and it was clear that I would not have to worry about being about being able to pay the court fees.

Out of the blue, John called in the middle of the night. I was half asleep when I picked up the phone. He announced that he was ready to talk. I was under the impression that he was nearly out of funds.

Nonetheless, I agreed to meet him at 2:00 a.m. in a secluded park. Against my better judgment, and worried that I was going to get mugged, I showed up. He acted amicably, pretending nothing had transpired between us. Questions about life kept popping up. I then confronted him and demanded to know why he wanted to meet.

It was the middle of the night and we were alone. I knew I could not trust him and we were by a semi-frozen lake. I realized how easy it would be for him to push me in and no one would be the wiser. I considered leaving but kept up with the chit-chat.

For over an hour we walked, with my feet freezing and concerned that my life might be in jeopardy. I think even he was confused about what he wanted to propose. A couple of times, he glared at me, and I wondered if perhaps he was considering solving his problem in a nefarious way.

I am sure he was swinging back and forth with what he was going to suggest. I made some jokes about how he must be running out of money, and how I had figured out how to move on. I also notified him that my girlfriend was aware I was out here with him and she was waiting for me to arrive home.

It was then that he brought up settling. I directed him to get his attorney to contact mine.

I could have tried pursuing him longer but it was clear the case would be drawn out for years. His entire argument in court relied on the fact that I had no paperwork proving my ownership of the websites or the funds. It was conveniently disregarded that this was because they were all locked up in the new office space that conveniently enough he refused to allow me access.

The problem was that I wanted my old websites back. We'd been going back and forth for nearly six months. I was mentally exhausted with the whole court proceedings and I wanted to move on. On top of that, if there was any hope of reviving my old websites, I would need to get them functional ASAP.

I cannot give the details of the legal settlement. What I can do is summarize. He would keep the money he stole, most of which has already been squandered in court fees. In exchange, I would acquire everything else, including 100% ownership of OmegaFX. To this day, it irks me that he avoided any fines or prison time. But at least I came out on top.

I took possession of all of the useless servers and hardware. Conveniently enough, around half of the hardware had magically disappeared, especially anything high-end. What remained, I sold on eBay. I would go back to working from home. Most importantly, I got back the websites.

Furthermore, I dissolved OmegaFX. It was an instant weight off my shoulders.

As I had guessed, the websites were pretty much dead in the eyes of the search engines. With not having court fees hanging over me, I decided I needed to invest in my new link exchange scheme. I requested that the company I used for outsourcing give me six full-time employees. Those employees then worked on finding link partners for all my old sites.

A month later, I moved that number up to nine employees.

I was relieved, as I had been under the impression that I had gotten lucky once and would never be able to regain what I'd lost. I had experienced one of the most stressful periods of my life. I was certain that my best days were behind me. It was difficult not to get depressed and throw in the towel, but perseverance had paid off.

It would take a long time for my income to recover to the post-OmegaFX days. I just had to be diligent and to keep creating new websites while churning out the link exchanges.

Luckily for me, I had my simple process and it worked remarkably well. As with almost anything I had tried on the internet, simple is almost always better. Never again would I return to doing things the hard way.

The sky was clearly the limit but my troubles would soon get worse. I had gotten access to all of my hardware and websites, but one thing was missing. All of my paperwork documenting my expenses, donations, and shareholder loans had been destroyed.

MOVING ON

I realized that it was time to move on. The opportunity for a new pay-per-click search engine was behind me. Even if I could do everything right the second time around, the market was far too advanced. AltaVista, GoTo, Dogpile, and myriad other lesser-known search engines were all gone in the dust. Now there was only Google....with Yahoo and Bing a distant second and third. Ask.com was managing to cling on to a 1% market share and had to spend hundreds of millions annually for this privilege.

I missed the opportunity. Looking back, I was simply too young and naïve. I made stupid mistakes that are so ridiculous they border on lunacy. In my defense, I had been nineteen years old when I registered OmegaFX. It's too bad that mistake would end up haunting me for much longer than even I could have anticipated.

Around this time, I decided I would focus on affiliate marketing, since it had clearly proven itself. If you find something that you are good at, you might as well capitalize on it. I started attending affiliate conferences. One memorable conference was Webmaster World, in Las Vegas. The attendance was huge and the founders of Yahoo threw a memorable party at a high-end nightclub. They rented blackjack tables that were spread out in the club and everyone was playing and competing for two hours, and whoever won the most money would win prizes.

I was never a good blackjack player, but since it was for fun, I decided that it could not hurt too much to cheat a little. When the person next to me spilled a drink and the dealer went to grab some napkins, I quickly dipped in and grabbed some extra chips. In the end, so many people ended up cheating (or giving away chips to friends) that they decided to make the draws random. After this, the tables were taken away and the party started.

Internet conferences, and most conferences for that matter, I rapidly discovered, are great tools for networking but you learn next to nothing. Information in the sessions is so basic that if you busied yourself with reading available information in books or forums, in less than two weeks you would know far more than they regurgitated. It didn't take long until I abandoned the sessions.

I found that if I could just negotiate a commission raise of 5% or 10% with one or two programs, it would pay for the whole trip and more.

One day I received an e-mail. An affiliate program offered to fly me for free to Australia. The trip was for five days. I asked if they could add 10 days of hotel stays and deduct it from my affiliate commission, and they agreed. I was flown for free, with my girlfriend, to Surfers Paradise in Queensland. I immediately started a love affair with Australia that would result in my returning three additional times.

I took two days to visit with the staff of the affiliate program. I toured the office and learned how they operated. Then, we explored the country for the rest of the trip.

The most productive trip was a free trip that I was awarded, along with ten of the best affiliates, to Belize. We stayed in an ocean-front lodge and networked for a week. During that period of time, we did horseback riding, hiking, as well as tubing in huge underwater caves. It was a memorable experience. I created lifelong friends among some huge heavy hitters in the affiliate industry.

Another free trip had top affiliates flown into San Jose, Costa Rica. We stayed at the Marriott for several days and we undertook multiple day trips, including one where they took us by catamaran to a secluded island. Most of the other affiliates played volleyball on the beach while I went out to explore the island and go swimming.

Another memorable free trip was to Las Vegas. An affiliate program brought in their top ten affiliates. They paid for the airfare, hotels, and far more. The highlight was when half of us were given a helicopter tour over the Grand Canyon. We stopped in the middle of nowhere for a picnic and then flew back to Las Vegas. Those days, affiliate programs were a lot more generous, as profit margins were larger.

The main problem with the internet is that the audience has only grown by maybe 30% while the competition has grown exponentially—I would estimate by as much as 1000%, in some industries.

So life went on. I focused on the internet business, attended some conferences and tried to increase my income. The problem was that I knew I would be hit with a HUGE tax bill. I didn't realize quite how huge. What I did know was that during the whole court process, I had to use every dollar that was rolling in to pay the lawyers. I did not have money to set aside for taxes, which were sitting at 41% at the time.

The larger problem was that I had no documents that outlined the business expenses for either me or OmegaFX, as John had destroyed them. He knew that if the papers were found, it could be evidence used against him and the lies in his affidavit.

So I tried to spend money conservatively. I did pay off more of the principal on my mortgage, but all the rest of the funds were being reserved toward my impending tax bill.

I ordered bank statements and my old credit card statements, and did everything else possible to recreate all of the expenses, but it was difficult.

Most internet businesses at the time did not provide hard copy receipts (they still don't) and all the accounting I had done was mysteriously missing.

And so the taxes were filed and I waited.

TAXES

One day, I received a phone call from the government. The woman on the other end sounded like she enjoyed destroying people. She threatened to take possession of my house unless the amount they assessed me was paid in full within a month. I hadn't even received the tax bill and all ready they were threatening me.

The amount they wanted was more money than I had earned since I started the internet business. I would be unable to write off all of the shareholder loans I made, as I had no proof of expenses for myself or OmegaFX.

I was also liable for the money John stole. He who earns the money is liable, not he who steals it. Worst of all, I could not prove that any of the Google AdWords advertising and GoTo advertising were legitimate business expenses

To keep things exciting, they charged me penalties and interest, which doubled the tax bill. I basically owed double of all I had earned, without being able to deduct anything. I managed some minor deductions that were pretty irrelevant in the grand scheme of things.

I could have tried going to court to fight it but I knew I could never prove my case. I read horror stories of people taking Revenue Canada to court and facing years of expenses… only to end up paying extra interest on the amount that was originally assessed.

I was really depressed about the whole situation. I had thought I could finally move on and that the worse was behind me.

It took about a day of being stressed out until I realized I had no choice. I would be living on the streets soon unless I declared bankruptcy, and so I visited a bankruptcy trustee.

At this point, it felt like I had worked my ass off for years and had next to nothing to show for it. I would go to conferences and watch successful affiliates living the high life. Here I was being conservative, and even worse, being completely honest with the Government of Canada and this was how they treated me.

I had always wanted to escape the brutal cold, the lack of sun for nine months a year, and the horrible taxes. This just reinforced my desire. I would not act on it until much later, but the seed was planted.

In the meantime, relocation was not an option, as I could not abandon my homeland with such a tax bill.

And so I quickly declared bankruptcy. It immediately froze the interest rates from growing and I was to be in bankruptcy for an "estimated" nine months. All my funds were used to pay the greedy government. They then wanted me to pay back the value of my car that exceeded $5000. Afterwards, they demanded an assessment on the value of my house and to pay back a certain amount on that. One major annoyance was the monthly statements I had to write out, which outlined personal expenses under categories such as groceries, power, health, and transportation.

But by far the most aggravating was that the whole time I was to be bankrupt, I would only be allowed to earn a maximum of $1800 per month.

Anything over this amount and I would pay a surplus income-tax rate.

So I paid the regular 41% income tax, and for anything over $1800, I would have to pay an additional 75% to the Canadian government. In reality, my tax rate was near 85%.

That meant that out of every $100,000 that I earned over my "surplus" income, I could keep a whopping $14,750.

It's very difficult to get motivated when a person pays an 85% income tax. I pretty much gave up on earning anything substantial. What was the point of my working? If I earned half a million, I could maybe keep $50,000. And on top of this, they wanted me to pay off the surplus that my car was worth and a surplus on the value of my house.

I really had no desire to work at this stage. To further create problems, when you are bankrupt you cannot own a credit card, which meant I could not advertise. In the United States, debit cards are attached to Mastercard and Visa. In Canada, debit cards are pretty much useless, as you cannot use them over the internet nor can you use them to check into a hotel room, rent a car, or anything else.

With no credit card, I essentially was unable to advertise. I would borrow a friend's credit card for flights and then pay the friend back in cash. But because it was not my credit card, I could not write off those expenses. I was therefore unable to grow my business and I watched it shrink considerably.

Link exchanges were starting to lose effectiveness and, on top of this, I had no way to pay my employees for further work. I decided to quit the link exchanges. Google was starting to discount reciprocal links. Reciprocal links is a glorified term for link exchanges.

My business was going south. My hands were tied behind my back; I had no money to advertise, and no money to invest. I would basically have to wait until the nine months were over. The only thing I did during this period was to attend a conference in Las Vegas, for which I had to use a friend's credit card to book, and it caused me major problems when checking in. It's a good thing I didn't have to rent a car, as I would have been unable to do so.

The saving grace was that, in theory, in nine months I could move on. I would have OmegaFX and Revenue Canada behind me.

The seed was planted for me to eventually leave the country. Even if I had a credit card, I would have been scared to use it, as I knew odds were that my expenses would not have been allowed for some ridiculous reason or another. From this point on, until I eventually left Canada, I tried to minimize expenses and potential advertising that could have created a large income. The lost opportunity cost was staggering.

My affiliate friend was considering moving out of Canada, so I decided to tag along on a trip to the Caribbean. I was seriously considering relocating when my financial predicament was over. The only problem was that I didn't know to where. My friend paid for the whole trip and I agreed that I could just repay him in the future once my troubles was over. I checked out the Grand Bahamas, as well as the Dominican Republic.

The Dominican Republic was a dual purpose trip. I had started dabbling in promoting on-line pharmacies. The commission was quite generous and it seemed like it was a market with pent-up demand. Americans were ordering pharmaceuticals from Canada, Mexico, India, and other countries that had price control laws. By ordering north of the border, Americans could save up to 90% off their prescription drugs.

I had been promoting lifestyle drugs such as Propecia, Viagra, Levitra, etc. When I heard there was a call center in Santa Domingo for an on-line pharmacy, it seemed like a good idea to visit to learn more.

What I learned from my visit to the call center turned me off on-line pharmacies. I did not realize the types of crooks who were involved in that industry. The call center people were trained to take orders for light pain killers and were then calling back the customers, trying to "upsell" them to addictive and dangerous pain killers that should absolutely require a doctor's prescription, such as Hydrocodone.

I quit the on-line pharmaceutical industry cold turkey. The Grand Bahamas was promising but was not quite my type of island. It might sound silly coming from a Canadian but I found the water was too cold. (If you are going to move to a tropical island, you want warm water.) Later, there happened to be a conference in Atlantis on Paradise Island, again in the Bahamas. I found that island was not what I was looking for either.

Since my funds were low, I was willing to try some new things. I had been flirting with the idea of promoting travel affiliate programs. I also wanted to travel, but money was tight, so I wanted somewhere with a direct flight.

It then dawned on me: I should do a short trip and create a small website for that destination in order to write off the expenses, as well as test out the travel market. I wanted something super simple and I decided to visit San Diego, based on the fact that it looked like a decent city, was nearby, warm, and the search volume for the city was quite significant.

I reviewed various affiliate programs. Hotels, airfare, and car rentals seemed too competitive. On top of this, they would have provided no legitimate reason to visit the city. Upon researching the city, I learned of a large number of world-class attractions, such as the San Diego Zoo and Sea World.

I also located an affiliate program that paid 10% commission for the sale of attraction passes. I then flew to San Diego, visited the attractions, and created the website http://www.sandiegoattractions.net. It was a simple, personalized write-up of the various attractions.

The funny thing is that the San Diego website started earning money nearly instantly, which actually surprised me. It earned a couple hundred a month for approximately five years, until Google decided to ban the website.

The ironic thing is that at the last minute, I decided against writing off the trip, as I didn't want Revenue Canada using it against me five years down the road. It was to be a recurring theme. Legally and technically, I could legitimately write off expenses but I was too scared to do so. I knew that if I wrote off something, I would receive a deduction for the year, but I also knew that three to five years down the road they could change their minds, which would result in having to pay back the deduction plus interest and whatever penalties they decided to impose that week.

And so my nine months of bankruptcy was nearing its end. Then, Revenue Canada decided to play hardball. They were making so much money off of me that they refused to allow me to exit my bankruptcy. It was one excuse after another.

After one year of lingering in bankruptcy and watching my income vanish into the 85% income tax bill, I had pretty much abandoned the business. There really was no point in working anymore. I still earned enough to live well but money was tight. I was pulling in around $30,000 a month, but once Revenue Canada took its share, it was all but gone. Every month the income would drop.

Instinctively I knew that I should work hard and have websites to generate cash once I was out of bankruptcy, but I just could not see an end in sight. Revenue Canada showed no mercy and was unwilling to release me. One thing I have learned is that you cannot fight the government; the only thing you can do is to relocate to a friendlier jurisdiction once you are able to do so.

How I wish I had moved out of Canada when the idea first struck. The lost income, the lost opportunity cost—it was in the millions.

Nine months of bankruptcy turned into a year, which turned into sixteen months, and then on the eighteenth month they finally released me.

The problem was that my income had dropped significantly. Once they finally released me, I was down to less than $10,000 a month. That was still a great amount of money, especially compared to what I could be earning from a regular job, but damn it, I had being earning more than ten times that at one point.

I still had no credit card, so I had to apply for one now that I was legally allowed to do so. Of course, only two secured credit cards were available in Canada. A secured credit card is a card into which you place funds as a security deposit. For instance, if you acquire a credit card for the value of $1000, you are required a make a $1000 security deposit. Once applied for, this secured credit card took two months before it was mailed out.

In those two months, my income dropped by half. I was now down to $5000 a month. I was lightly entertaining the possibility that I might have to acquire a regular job. With the current slide, I would be down to $1000 a month in less than 90 days. I had gone from riches to average income, and I knew poverty was a possibility.

I was using my girlfriend's credit card to pay for hosting and domain name renewals. I was unable to write these expenses off as they were under her name. Also, since they were monitoring her income, we could not do anything to increase it as this would raise a flag. This was the cost of doing business in Canada.

Finally, once I had received the secured credit card, I could start paying for stuff. At first, it was just domain name renewals and hosting, as I was paranoid about spending money on advertising. The last thing I wanted was to have my business expenses denied. I saw many opportunities that I could have taken but ignored them for this reason.

The next two years were pretty slow and my growth was pretty stagnant.

My income was increasing slowly, but it was not nearly at the former levels. Slowly, I grew courageous enough to start spending money on the business. I vowed there would be no more mistakes, and no more large screw-ups like OmegaFX and the Revenue Canada fiasco.

I knew I would soon need to make a big move. I had to find the next big score, something that would allow me an advantage over the competition in the same way that the link exchanges had achieved. I saved up all my income, which started growing slowly. I knew I would have to invest in something that offered a guaranteed SEO advantage. The problem was that I didn't know what it would be.

POKER FORUM

Around this time, I used up my savings and bought a popular poker forum with NeverBeg.com. The idea with the poker forum was to promote poker affiliate programs. Whenever someone plays a hand of poker, a small percentage is taken for the house. This is called the "rake." An affiliate would receive approximately a quarter of the rake.

The problem was that the amount of work involved was stupendous. I could see room for growth, but after one month of having to babysit forum users and ridiculous flame wars, as well as idiotic he said/she said e-mails, I decided it was not worth the stress.

The other problem with the forum I bought was that it catered to deadbeat poker players. Some of the members might have been excellent players, but they were unable to manage their own money. They would then get other players to "stake" them. Staking was especially popular with tournaments, which required larger entry fees.

And so I had a forum with deadbeat players who would essentially "beg" one another for money to play poker. Hence the name of the site: Never Beg. Unfortunately, these type of players loved causing problems. Many of them frequented the website up to twelve hours a day between hands of poker. If I had purchased a forum in which I enjoyed the company of the members, I might have decided to keep it, but this was certainly not the case.

I had earned a small income, but decided to sell the site and obtain a tiny capital gains. My return on investment was approximately 10% in a one-month period. Basically Never Beg was a time hog, and I had to choose between it and all my other sites. I chose the sites that involved the least amount of work. It was good riddance to Never Beg.

Approximately a year ago, I was talking to a friend of mine and he brought up NeverBeg.com. Apparently, it was later sold to third party and he estimated the site value to be in the high six figures. Most people would be angry at themselves. Nonetheless, I knew that had I focused my energy on the forum, the opportunity cost would have been in *the millions. Even if I did lose out on a potential profit of $500,0000+, I do not regret the decision to sell. We each have to pick our own wars.*

PRIVATE LABELING

I attempted one last time to have my own product line. I located a wholesaler in the United States that offered in-house label printing with no minimum orders. These were herbal products, and the wholesaler would drop ship them once I e-mailed them my list of customers. The bottles were mailed out with my product name, as well as my company name on the mailing slips.

I had a number of health sites that started to rank extremely well in Yahoo. I featured the herbal products on these sites. The theory was that my margins would be higher. I earned approximately 10% more per order. Unfortunately, to earn that 10% involved a lot of work, such as customer service, tracking shipments, and optimizing the conversions of landing pages.

Over the next three months, I realized that to earn that extra 10% percent was simply a ridiculous nonproductive waste of time. The amount of money I spent on designs ripped apart that 10%. This basically meant that I was working for free. It was more efficient to just send customers directly to merchants that specialized in these industries. The merchants would have specialists that could offer better customer support, as well as top designers and marketers to optimize landing pages and sales copy.

After three months I decided that it was not worthwhile to keep the private label. Yahoo had also dropped my best performing health websites, so the amount of traffic I was receiving was down exponentially.

I contacted the wholesaler and called it quits. On a good note, I lost no money. What was important was that the experience simply reinforced that it made no sense for me to have my own product. Being an affiliate created far less stress, as well as allowing me to maximize earnings by being able to focus 100% exclusively on marketing and search engine optimization. This was far more effective than dividing my time between customer service, design issues, shipping, private labels, etc.

THE POWER OF A DOLLAR

And so we can fast forward to 2007. I decided to move to Vancouver and lived five minutes away from a friend who was also an affiliate. Moving really helped motivate me to regain my lost drive. We would toss ideas back and forth.

My income had still never fully recovered from my bankruptcy days. I was still looking for the next big score.

Link exchanges were dead, but Google still valued links over anything else. It was quite comical: At one time, I witnessed an on-line pharmacy site ranking #1 for the term "online casino." How did this happen? The owner had spammed links with automated software. He had screwed up his software settings and had links going to his online pharmacy site with the term "online casino," and his casino site had been spammed with links for the term "online pharmacy." It clearly showed that content was next to irrelevant. In the meantime, Google was still lying to webmasters and claiming that content was the most important attribute of their website.

Up until this day, I would speculate that content is less than 15% of what Google evaluates. They focus primarily on what website is linking to you.

This is when I started noticing something that would drive my income through the roof again and return me to former levels.

I had always purchased links at directories. A paid directory is simply somewhere at which you pay the directory and they list your website under a specific category. But now, there was a new type of directory on the market. It was the bidding directory. The concept was simple. The more you bid, the higher your site listing under the specific category. Bids almost always started at $1.

I speculated that a $1 link would hold the same value to Google as the $500 link. Even if the $500 link was placed first in the relevant category, it could not be that much more valuable. After all, the links were coming from the same source, so who cares which link was listed higher.

And so I pulled the trigger on this new idea to build links. This was my ONLY marketing strategy at the time. I deposited money into PayPal and bought thousands of links and would bid only $1. My sites all started to increase in search engine rankings. All of a sudden, I had top 5 rankings again, and in some instances I was number 1

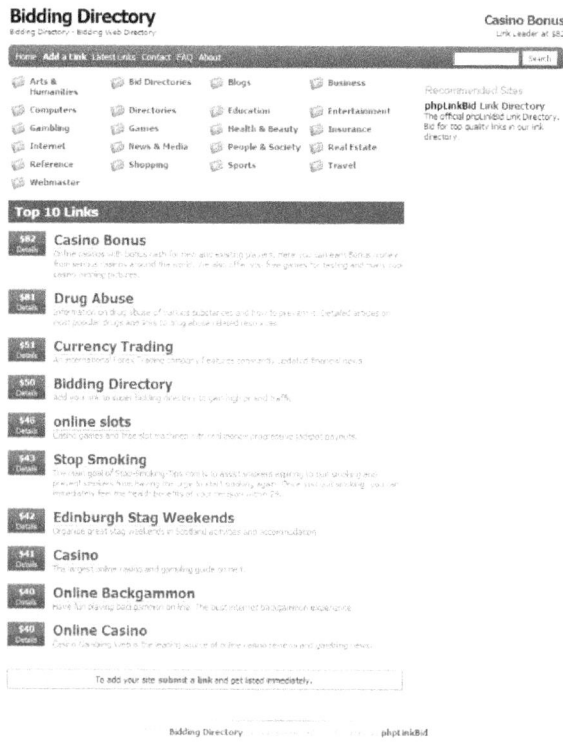

I now had an easy recipe for success, a formula that I could duplicate.

My Formula:

1. Create a five page website to target a specific search term.

2. Buy $1 directory links.

3. Keep buying links until the website has a top five search engine ranking.

4. Repeat the above.

Just like that I was back in business. I created new sites and bought links for all of my old sites that I knew would be the most profitable. My income exploded exponentially, along with the increase in search-engine rankings. Within a month I was back in the game, with a 1000% increase in income over what it had been less than six months ago.

Several months passed and I allowed the income to roll in, while always setting aside half for taxes.

How many $1 directory links did I buy? It depended on how competitive the search term was. Sometimes it only required a few hundred and sometimes a few thousand. At one point, I ran out of directories to bid on.

This technique was genius in its simplicity. I was shocked that almost no one else was taking advantage of it. You could see the changes in the Google search results as soon as you purchased links. For instance, if I bought 100 $1 directory links, I might be 30th under a certain search term. If I bought another 100 links, suddenly I would be 20th. Once I hit 500 directories, I would be in the top 10. If I bought every single $1 directory link I could find, I would most likely find myself in the top 5 for the search term I was targeting.

This was more expensive than link exchanges, but it was a guaranteed way of generating links. I would speculate that this worked with 90% of my websites. If I invested $1000, my site would show up in the top 10.

I had finally discovered something that I could go "all in" on. I capitalized on it and had one of my best years.

I also saved up all that money, and would be paying cash for something huge.

A BIG MOVE

In the previous year or two, I had checked out numerous locations to potentially relocate to. I had toured Costa Rica, Belize, and Barbados, amongst others. Unfortunately, none really struck my fancy. Another affiliate contacted me and informed me he was checking out Grand Cayman and asked if I wanted to tag along.

My on-line research had me initially dismissing the Cayman Islands as being too difficult to relocate to. Nonetheless, I agreed to check it out.

I met up with him in Grand Cayman. From the first moment that I landed, I knew I could live here. There was almost no crime or poverty compared to the rest of the Caribbean. The island was relatively safe and clean, especially by Caribbean standards. Best of all, the ocean was amazing. I always longed to live by the ocean in a tropical climate. And unlike the Bahamas, the water was super warm.

My second day on the island, I visited an attorney to inquire about moving here. I was shocked at how simple it was. This attorney assisted me in forming a corporation that would issue me a work visa.

Day three I paid cash for a condo on Seven Mile Beach. I could thank the bidding directories for this.

This was my moment, I was sick of the way that Canada treated me, sick of the snow, sick of being afraid to invest in my business, exhausted from being taken advantage of. I could now start living somewhere that had ZERO income tax. I could also save on the expense and hassle of hiring an accountant. How much I earned was my own business; I did not have to file taxes. I could now live on my own terms and live in a virtual paradise.

It was quite ironic that when I returned to Canada four days later, I encountered the front door being wide open. My house had been emptied. Someone had robbed it clean, even going so far as stealing my blanket. They took all the electronics, DVDs, television, telescope—pretty much everything. And to top it off, they even stole my car. It was quite the twist of fate, as I had been worrying about what to do with all my assets.

I got the car back from the police several weeks later, which I then had to worry about selling.

I stayed in Canada for several months, tying loose ends and preparing my house to be sold.

And that was the end of Canada and taxes for me. I flew to the Caymans with two suitcases and never had to pay one more cent of income tax.

GEOTARGETTING

It was now 2008 and I was overlooking the calm sea from my ocean-front condo. Life was good. I no longer worried about taxes and I had abandoned my obsession with work. The priority was to travel and enjoy life.

I wanted something simple that would enable me to do this. I gave myself six months to figure out future income streams. The $1 bidding directories were no longer effective. It was too easy a loophole, and Google modified the algorithm to disregard bidding directories.

Nonetheless, I could rank for semi-competitive terms by submitting websites to legitimate directories. What makes a directory legitimate? Basically, anything that has some type of human review system in place.

What I quickly noticed is that this was not enough to get me a ranking in the top ten for super-competitive keywords. Something else I noticed is that every English webmaster in the world was pretty much targeting the United States. I had always done well with the United States, but the competition was getting a bit fierce. I could still rank well but with effort I was not willing to apply.

And so I created five-page websites that would target Canada, the UK,

South Africa, and Australia. I was going after countries with less competition. A five-page website going after a competitive term in those countries usually required fewer than 20 links from directories to rank well. At least that was the case with Canada, South Africa, and Australia. I quickly gave up on the UK as it was too competitive, and when I ranked, the traffic was too little to justify all the work.

Geotargetting was doing well and continues to do so. Currently, 80% of my income is from outside the United States and the United Kingdom.

After I decided I would focus on geotargetting, I realized I had been stupid all along. I would need to reevaluate my relationship with domain names.

DOMAIN NAMES

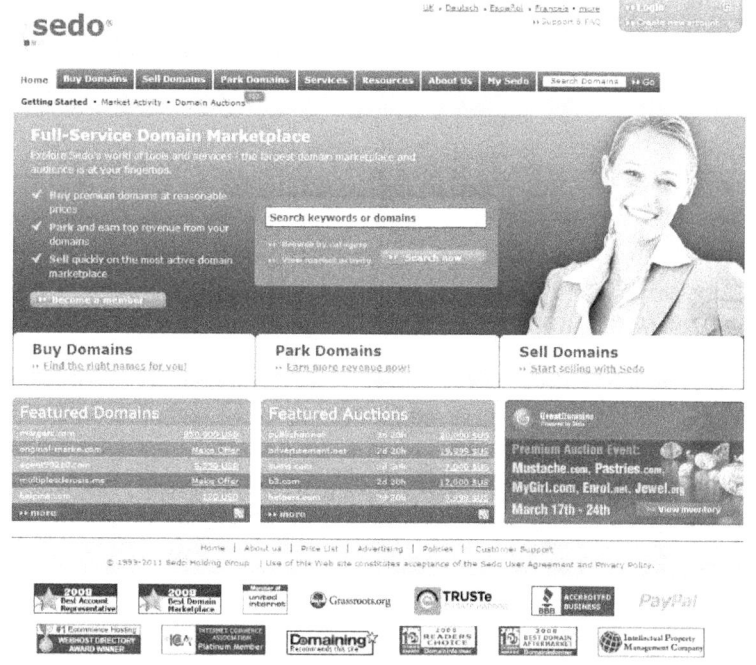

After undertaking a lot of research, it was evident that keyword-specific domain names had a huge advantage over ordinary domain names. It is

Google's way of forcing a "cost of entry" on the little guy that ensures that only websites with some level of investment rank well.

And so I started to buy keyword-specific domains. For instance, if I wanted to target the keyword "Dating websites" for Canada, I would buy datingwebsites.ca or dating-websites.ca (in this instance I got the second name in the example).

By getting keyword-specific domains, the odds of ranking for a specific term were significantly increased. I cannot possibly stress enough how much getting the right domain name helps. It's something I wish I had figured out when I first started. For instance, in the past I would have registered safedatingwebsites.ca instead of going for dating-websites.ca. This was the wrong approach. By getting the specific keyword domain for the search term you are going after, it is five to ten times easier to rank for a search query.

I even started going after some search terms in the United States as long as I could get a good domain name. All the good domains were taken for the United States, so I would buy names off sedo.com. Sedo is hands-down the largest domain name marketplace in the world.

How do I know it's that much easier to rank well with a good domain name?

During those first six months in Grand Cayman, I did a lot of testing. Reading on SEO forums would not cut it. I needed to test out different SEO strategies personally. This is what I learned about the power of domain names.

The examples below are to rank for the term dating websites for people searching from Canada.

Datingwebsites.ca would rank easier than dating-websites.ca because Google dislikes dashes. One dash is good; anything more is bad.

Dating-websites.ca is far superior than canadadatingwebsites.ca or datingwebsitescanada.ca.

Datingwebsitescanada.ca is far superior than canadadatingwebsites.ca. If Google sees the search term first in the domain name, it gives it more value. How much more value? I would estimate it takes 50% fewer links.

When it came to geotargetting, some other things were important.

In Google UK, .co.uk and .org.uk are of equal value. This is important because .org.uk domains are often still available or else much cheaper on Sedo.

The .me.uk domain extensions are next to impossible to rank well on Google. Google hates this extension.

For instance, I had the .org.uk and .me.uk for the exact same term. The .org.uk took five times fewer links to rank in the top 10, while the .me.uk had a difficult time breaking the top 100. Everything else was equal; even the links were coming from the same source. Furthermore, the content was of similar or nearly identical quality.

For the United States, .com, .net, .org, and eventually .co, when it was released, could all rank with significantly less effort than other domain extensions.

The .info, .us, .ws, .me, and similar extensions automatically will struggle to rank well in Google. This is especially true with .info. Do not acquire these domain extensions, as Google will make it next to impossible to rank, regardless of how much great content you create. By buying an .info, it will take ten times more work to get the same result as a .com, .net, .org, or .co.

This is the power of domain names. Eventually I learned that the UK was not worth targeting. The United States was only worth targeting if I could get the keyword-specific domain name that I desired. For instance, I bought http://www.ufcbetting.net, as it was a perfect keyword match to a great search term.

The power of a domain name did not hit me until one day when I had the opportunity of purchasing the perfect name for a keyword I had being targeting for years. My old domain, to which I had built links for years, was in the top 40. After launching the perfect keyword domain, I was ranking in the top 10 for that same search query within one week. I hit top 10 with less than 5% of the number of links and with far less content than my original website.

The only links I purchased were directory links. I could only find about 20 good directories, so that's all I bought. Eventually I started to go to wlmarketing.com to buy press releases, social bookmarking, and article links.

My marketing strategy as I write this is still the same. Above, I outlined the secrets to my current success. It's a recipe that is easy to follow.

After the six months of rethinking my strategies, and for the next three years, I would travel for approximately nine months a year. This included going to Canada in the summer to visit friends and do some hiking. Here's an example of one of my trips:

Fly into Australia for 45 days, fly into Hawaii for 3 weeks, fly into Miami, Florida for 4 days, and then fly into Trinidad for some volunteer work for 10 days, fly to Costa Rica to inspect a boutique hotel I was buying into, and then return home for 2 weeks before flying to Canada.

I was finally living the life of my dreams. I vowed that I would have the internet working for me and not work on the internet. There is a vast difference. I have turned down many opportunities because they were too time-consuming.

If a website requires a lot of work, I know it is not for me. I want the ability to launch a website and to have the website sit in cyberspace and to forget about it. I do not want to update anything. This is why I refuse to partake in the rush for "social marketing." I do not find it efficient to Twitter for hours each day or to make Facebook friends. Those methods cannot be scaled, which is why I ignore them.

I also gave up on going after super-competitive terms in the United States. It requires too much effort that I do not wish to commit to.

CHARITY REVISITED

After relocating to the Cayman Islands, something was bothering me. I had started Sportula with the intention of raising money for charity. Unfortunately, the project ended up being a financial disaster. Nonetheless, I still wanted to do something worthwhile. I was still donating to charity on a monthly basis but I wanted to do something more public that would trigger others to also give.

I was talking to a good friend of mine who specializes in press releases when he mentioned that he could offer me a free press release, as he was doing this for a current on-line casino by the name of Slot Land that was busy funding schools in Malawi. I had donated funds to this project in the past and it was a project started by a grassroots organization.

I strongly believe that grassroots organizations are the future of charitable giving. While huge nonprofits, like Doctors Without Borders, do a lot of good, grassroots organizations have the potential to integrate into a community to change its course.

BoNGO was established in 1997 and was a grassroots organization that focused on Malawi. They offered preschool education and teacher training, as well as undertaking other important projects.

And so I decided to combine charitable giving with a website that generated profits in order to motivate other affiliates to donate. Below are some of the press release.

CasinoRanking.com Donates a Year of Commissions to Slotland's African Aid Project

July 8, 2008 (London, UK) -- Now that the school and community center that it built in Malawi is fully self-sustaining, online casino Slotland.com is concluding its funding. To date, the online slot machine and video poker site has donated more than $100,000 to construct the much needed facilities and train teachers and staff. As the local Project Team moves on to assist other villages another online gambling leader, CasinoRanking.com, has stepped forward to donate at least $10,000 toward ongoing projects.

For more than two years, the popular online slot machine and video poker web site, Slotland.com, provided all funding required to construct buildings and train local teachers in the remote and impoverished village of Juma, Malawi. The goal of the African aid project has always been that it should be self-sustaining and since the Project Team built a maize mill to generate ongoing revenue, the centre has required minimal outside funding.

But the work of the Project Team isn't finished. The centre has become a teacher-training center for the region and continues to help other schools in the region get established and improve their teaching methods. The Team has also become involved in the construction of other self-sustaining community projects like a maize mill in Kantimbanye that now provides income for the school in Juma.

"We've learned that self-initiated projects are most likely to succeed," said the Project Team Leader, David Leflar. "Where there's a will, we will help them find a way!"

"The school that we've funded will have a long lasting benefit to the entire community. It provides opportunities and will help end the cycle of poverty in Malawi," said Martin Smith of Slotland. "We're very proud that one of our biggest affiliates, CasinoRanking.com, was impressed enough with the positive results of our project that they're making a very substantial donation of their own."

"The online casino business is a high profit industry," said Antoine of CasinoRanking.com. "We should consider ourselves lucky to have the opportunity to help others who are not as fortunate."

"I understand that the school is now completed," said Antoine, "But Malawi is still one of the poorest nations on earth. If the money can go towards building wells or finding clean water that would be great too. Obviously we can trust this dedicated Project Team to decide how to best spend the money."

The story of how the Project Team brought a whole village together to build the Umodzi-Mbame School is told on a fundraising website provided by Slotland: www.help-malawi-children-charity.org. The site also explains how donations will be used by the African charity to assist neighboring villages that have started similar projects on their own. Donations toward current and new projects can be made on the site through secure PayPal payment processing.

ENDS

For further information please contact:

Larry Colcy

(604) 685-6240

Slotland@lyceummedia.com

About Bongo Malawi

boNGO Worldwide, NFP, is a Malawian non-governmental, non-profit organization established in 2007 by four volunteers -- the Project Team members from the USA, Switzerland, Czech Republic, and Malawi. boNGO is an acronym for "Based On Need-driven Grassroots Ownership". Intense cooperation with two very different rural communities led the Project Team towards the realization that one of the most important factors when implementing positive and sustainable development is choosing the right partner. The Project Team works only with villages that yern for their own transformation, have their own visions, and are actively trying to achieve them. boNGO Worldwide accepts donations through its fundraising website, Help-Malawi-Children-Charity.org.

About Slotland.com

Established in 1998, Slotland.com is renowned for its fairness, security and sincerity. Slotland.com's progressive jackpot is currently won on average every six weeks and usually stands at over $100,000, making it one of the most frequently won jackpots on the Internet. In 2005, the pioneering entertainment company introduced its first slot machine for the mobile phone/PDA platform. Slotland.com has been voted "Most Unique Slot Site" and "Best Progressive Jackpot Site" by Strictly Slots Magazine readers, named "Best Web TV" in a Gambling Online Magazine poll, and selected as a finalist in the ME Awards "Best Mobile Gambling Company" category.

About CasinoRanking.com

CasinoRanking.com, a leading source for online casino gaming information, publishes reviews and recommends online casinos, poker rooms, bingo and sportsbetting sites. Their Top 30 List ranks online casinos considering graphics, software, customer support and ease/speed of collecting winnings. The website also offers casino rankings for multiple languages/countries.

Later on, this additional press release was sent out:

Affiliate Site Donates $30,000 to Malawi Charity

Leading online casino affiliate site CasinoRanking.com has donated three years of commissions to a charity dedicated to improving the lives of children in the small African nation of Malawi.

CasinoRanking.com has given boNGO Worldwide, a non-profit organization created by a small group of American and Czech aid workers, more than $30,000 to help it operate a school and nearby maize mill that provides revenues for the local community.

Innovative online slots and video poker site Slotland.com donated over $100,000 to boNGO in 2005 to help build the school, which has gone on to become a training centre for the area's primary school teachers and serve as a model of sustainable development.

"After the initial year of funding for the Malawi project was complete, it was just clear to me that boNGO had much more work to do so I kept the funding up," said Antoine from CasinoRanking.com.

"I find that grass-root organizations are much more effective than larger non-profits. Large organizations seem to waste a lot on non-essentials such as office space and fund raising."

The school recently saw 42 children graduate and boNGO has continued its efforts by establishing a further 13 education and community-based childcare centers in Africa with trained teachers.

"One of the big focuses with boNGO has been on teaching sustainability, which I personally find is important," said Antoine.

"A delicate balance between development and sustainability needs to be maintained to ensure the future of Malawi and its people."

Antoine is challenging casino affiliate webmasters to consider contributing to this very worthy cause and stated that more information about its recent and current projects can be found at boNGOWorldwide.com

One day, while checking the mail, I had pleasant surprise. Someone had sent me a painting of both the school and the children who attended it. I still have the painting in my bedroom.

VALUES

One valuable insight that I learned over the years: My time is more important than money. I do not work for money. I work for the freedom to use my time as I yearn to. I know money can disappear overnight. I also know that one thing that cannot be changed is how much time I have left on this planet. Each one of us has a finite lifespan. Each day that is gone is a day lost. I refuse to be a slave to my computer, to the taxman, or to anyone specific.

Over the years, I watched my money vanish in front of my eyes. A lot of it could be attributed to pure stupidity, a lot to bad luck. Regardless, I now know that I do not want money ruling over me.

I watched some affiliates who were rolling in six figures a month become slaves to money. They did not work for freedom; they worked for money. One poor affiliate, and I call him that not because he had a lack of income, was working 15 hours a day for years. He was classified as a super-affiliate and earned six figures a month. His weight ballooned out of control. That affiliate owned a mansion and five cars, and he also had five children that he left behind after suffering a heart attack. This affiliate was barely forty.

The danger of having too much money is in becoming addicted to it. I started off addicted to money and the ironic thing is that I ended up losing all of it because of this. It's not until I started living my dreams that things got better. I moved to the tropical paradise that I always dreamed of. The secondary benefit is that there was no income tax. The main benefit was the ocean, the warm water, and never having to shovel or to ask my neighbor to help push my car out of a snow bank.

My income soared when I started working less. A lot of that is luck while a lot of it was just pure refusal to do anything that required too much time. I bought myself freedom. Not paying taxes also meant that my income automatically doubled over night.

I've been to Hawaii three times now, and each time spent three weeks on a beautiful island. I've been to Australia three times since moving here. Last time I was there, I hiked 90 kilometers on the Great Ocean Walk. It was great exercise and a life-changing experience. In the Caribbean I've been able to visit nearby islands such as Jamaica, Cuba, Trinidad (where I got to volunteer working hands-on with Leatherback sea turtles), St. Martin, and a beautiful gem of an island called Saba (you should look it up). I traveled Europe extensively for a 6-week period. I've also seen a lot of North America and Central America. Next I am focusing on South America, and afterwards, the sky is the limit.

I rarely launch new websites these days, even when I discover opportunities with keyword-specific domain names. To me, the end goal is not to make as much money as possible. I have seen people who do this and who end up being slaves to money, as I once was. That is no longer my goal. I have moved on from that stage in life.

For most people, work is the most restrictive and time-consuming task they undertake. They work five days a week for two days of freedom. Every hour worked equals only one hour of income. The internet allows people the ability to catapult themselves past these restrictive limitations.

One hour of income for one hour of work can never be leveraged. This is why you need to become a boss and own a business. I could leverage the power of websites. If I had one website doing well and I wanted a tenfold increase in income, I could then create ten similar websites. Can you possibly work ten times more? No, it's impossible. The best you can hope for is a small increase of up to twenty percent and that is being generous. On top of this, working all the time is not healthy.

I found my catapult with the internet. Now I am leveraging it for my non-internet-related activities.

What I desire is to buy the freedom to use my time in the way that I want. From 2008 to 2011, I piled up my money while watching the recession hit North America. I waited and waited until the time was right to invest my funds and allow my money to work for me.

INVESTMENTS

I watched the real estate market collapse. I was lucky that I did not have funds tied up in real estate but I also knew it was an opportunity of a life time to move on.

I ended up buying real estate all over the world, but what I wanted was freedom, and so I bought myself freedom. I bought a small villa in a boutique resort in Costa Rica that has been featured in international travel magazines such as *Condé Nast Traveler*.

Then one day I received an interesting offer. The owners of the resort in Costa Rica intended to sell the resort, but if possible, they wanted to sell it to current villa owners. This was just one month after I had purchased an individual villa.

I contemplated my future. I had wanted to diversify for nearly a decade. And so I decided to buy out the resort and to become the majority shareholder.

I bought condos in Brazil, Europe, the United States, and even Panama. I even bought into a development in Tanzania.

Websites were initially my leverage, but after working on the internet for over a decade, it's time to experience different things.

And so my new leverage is real estate. This has afforded me the freedom to no longer worry about the internet. Regardless, my affiliate sites are still generating a large income stream. Every once in a while, I see a great domain name opportunity so I buy that domain name and launch a new five-page website. I refuse to spend much time on a website and I do all of the SEO in one day.

Compared to most webmasters, one day of SEO might be considered blasphemy. One day of SEO is not enough to rank well by using my strategy for the gold keywords in the United States or the United Kingdom. Regardless, it is enough to allow me to rank well for secondary money terms in these markets and to rank well for most money terms in Canada and Australia.

I prefer to lose out on some opportunities in order to enjoy what is important to me instead. Once upon a time, I would not have made a similar decision, I am glad I now have the luxury to be picky.

Why am I willing to give away my recipe? I have bought all the domain names that I wanted in Canada, Australia, and the United States. On top of this, I have very little desire to develop more websites. If a good opportunity knocks, I'll take it.

Then again…with thirteen years of doing this, it's time for me to move on.

MY CURRENT RECIPE

1. Use the Google Keyword Tool:

Go to https://adwords.google.com/select/KeywordToolExternal. Once this page has loaded, you search for keywords in the industry that you wish to target. Google displays searches that have a high volume. Make sure you click on "exact" under "match types" and uncheck the "broad" box.

The broad box is a really a useless parameter and the most common mistake people make is leaving this checked. For instance, if you search "Costa Rica Hotels," if you had "broad" selected, it would indicate that over 100,000 people search that term every month. The reality is that over 100,000 people had searched terms that included some of the words in that query—for instance, "Costa Rica," "Cheap Costa Rica Hotel," or "San Jose Costa Rica Hotel." Either way; ensure you select "exact" to get an accurate picture.

If you wish to dig a bit deeper, under "advanced options and filters" specify the location of searches. That way, if you create a website for Canada, you will know how many times a specific query is searched from Canada. The same applies for any country.

You can also use http://www.wordtracker.com instead of the Google

Keyword Tool.

You'll view a list of search terms. Now open up your favorite domain-name registrar and look up which term is available.

2. Exact keyword domains:

To make it easy on yourself and to end up doing ten times less work for the exact same result, you NEED an exact keyword domain. Of course, this is not always possible, but it is ideal. Check if the extensions .com, .net, .org, or .co are available (in that order). If they are not available, then search again but add a hyphen (-) in the middle.

For instance, I bought dating-websites.com instead of datingwebsites.com. If you are geotargeting countries such as Canada or Australia, you must be a resident or a citizen in those countries to register the appropriate domain name extension. For instance, you need to be Canadian to register .ca, or Australian to register .com.au. If you cannot register these, do not despair, as Google analyzes more than the domain name extension.

Also, there is a way to bypass these restrictions. It is more of an investment, but if you form a corporation in these jurisdictions, that corporation can then own the appropriate domain name.

If you cannot register the country-code domain extension, it is not the end of the world. Since ranking in Canada, Australia, and South Africa is so easy, just add the word Canada, Australia, or SA (or South Africa) to your domain name. For instance, datingwebsitescanada.org would be good. Remember to have your keyword first, as that domain is better than canadadatingwebsites.org.

The secondary benefit of this is when searchers locate your website in the search results; they know instantly that you cater to their demographic. People always prefer to frequent a website that is designed specifically for the country in which they reside.

If you still cannot locate a good domain name, try visiting http://www.sedo.com. This is a domain name marketplace where you can purchase a domain name from a reseller. If the domain name is not for sale for a reasonable amount, or you do not wish to invest this much capital, simply move on to the next search query. I sometimes look up 300 search terms before finding a good domain candidate, so do not lose hope. Investing time in domain name research saves a ton of work (and money) later on.

Also bear in mind that in some countries, you can register the domain names, even if you do not reside there. For instance, you can register .co.uk and .org.uk even if you are not a UK citizen or resident.

3. Geotargeting Hosting:

Your domain name is registered. Congratulations! If you bought a country-specific domain extension, you can skip this step.

Now you want to inform Google about the country your website was designed for. You achieve this by hosting the domain name in the country you are targeting. For example, if you have datingwebsitescanada.org, you would host the website in Canada. This tells Google that the site is relevant to Canadians. Make sure you host in the correct country; this is extremely important. If not, you can inform Google of what country you are targeting in Google Webmaster Tools (http://www.google.com/webmasters/tools/), but I firmly believe it's best to host in the country you are targeting.

Of course, hosting in the specific country is not always an option; it is simply preferable. Who should you use for a webhost? Search from google.com.au for webhosts if you want an Australian host, from google.ca for a Canadian host, etc. Or else, see the tools section at the end of this book to view my recommended list of webhosts.

4. Launch the Website:

Create or outsource your website. Personally I am lazy and do not want to work, so I outsource everything.

I use:

- http://www.freelancer.com
- http://www.elance.com
- http://www.guru.com

If you want something that is really state of the art, try http://www.99designs.com. 99 Designs is more expensive and I use it for websites from which I expect a lot of traffic or are important in another way. With 99 Designs, you submit a website request and award a monetary prize. Web designers then submit mockups and you then can pick a winner and the prize is awarded to this person.

When it comes to web design, personally I find that simple is better. Of course, you may choose a different strategy. Personally, I create five-page websites that I never have to update. I don't even specify the year in the copyright information so as to avoid updating this annually. I do this because I am lazy.

Google does appreciate fresh content more and more. If you want a blog on your website that you can update with a small post every week or two, this is very beneficial. I don't need to do this, so I avoid it, but I KNOW my income would go up if I updated my sites regularly with fresh content.

I recommend that you create fresh content especially when starting out. I do not use blogs but if you want to add one to your website, simply search "blog software" or a similar term in Google.

While fresh content is important, I urge you not to overcomplicate your website. Launch something quickly, and once you are ranking, you can worry about adding nifty and interactive tools if you absolutely need to.

To create content, I sometimes use http://www.textbroker.com. I also sometimes use them to have professional writers create press releases and to write articles for submission to article websites.

5. Submit to Directories:

I submit to a network of directories that I reuse for all of my websites. I use American directories for all my sites and then I use the Australian, Canadian, and UK directories when appropriate to do so (basically if I am targeting that country.)

I keep a list of directories here:
http://www.dotaffiliate.com/directories.html

Also I submit to topic-specific directories. For example, if launching a dating website, I try to list my website with the top dating directories. The same applies with a financial website: I would then target financial directories, and so forth.

6. Other Marketing Tools:

If you are launching an important website and legitimately expect to have newspapers and magazines pick up your press release, use http://www.prweb.com to submit press releases.

If you have a simple affiliate website or something that is not as newsworthy, use http://www.wlmarketing.com or a similar service. These outsourcers can submit your article/press release to the relevant sources. They can also use social bookmarking. What this means is they will hire someone to bookmark your website on close to 100 social networks. These count as very weak links.

I wait to see if the above techniques have worked. If not, after a month, I will use http://www.submitedge.com, which offers sneakier (black hat) ways of gathering links.

That's it: that's the formula. I can sit down, buy a domain name, outsource the design, and create all of the written content in 2 to 3 hours. I then submit the website to directories for another 2 hours and then I outsource the rest.

Even typing this, I am shocked at how simple my system is and how overly complicated most webmasters make things. Why work more than you have to?

I do believe that outsourcing is a huge time-saver and I recommend that you outsource unless you absolutely cannot afford it. Once your website is complete, try submitting it to http://www.dmoz.org. The odds of getting listed are low. If you notice there are no editors in your category and you are interested in the topic, then volunteer to become an editor. Don't reveal that you are volunteering to submit your website, but do submit it if they accept you as an editor. Being listed in Dmoz gives you a huge boost in Google and other search engines.

PENGUINS

I was in the process of launching this book and had just finished writing the "secret recipe" when on April 24, 2012, Google decided to launch the nicknamed "Penguin Update."

At first I cursed. I will be honest: a lot of my sites, especially the ones prior to 2008, got hit hard. The website that was involved in the press releases was essentially banned and cannot be found under the keywords it was targeting.

And so I waited and wanted to do some testing. I am happy to report that not much has changed.

Up until the first half of 2012, my strategy worked perfectly and it's still functional. The only difference is that from 2008 to April, 2012, I could use one anchor text (title keyword that links to my site) such as dating websites (for dating-websites.com or dating-websites.ca) and Google would love this. Now, Google has the "penguin" overoptimization penalty. All this means is that to avoid the penguin penalty, you need to use different anchor texts instead of the same one repeatedly.

I therefore recommend that you use the exact keyword anchor text less than fifty percent of the time. For instance, if I were launching http://www.dating-websites.ca today, I would use the anchor text "dating websites" five out of ten times. The other half of the time, I would mix it up and use the following anchor texts: dating websites Canada, dating website, dating-websites.ca, Canadian dating websites, etc. The bonus with this strategy is that you might start ranking for some secondary search terms.

This is the only difference with the Penguin update. If you vary your anchor text, you shouldn't need to worry about it. As for on-page SEO, it is more important than ever to make it seem like you are not doing SEO. That means you should only mention your keyword in the text of the website as many times as you need to.

I would love to tell you more about what you should do, but the reality is that I've outlined all 100% of my strategy. Now you have to use what you know about the world, and incorporate the parts of my formula that you consider useful into your own internet strategy. My formula was created to promote affiliate programs. Perhaps you can use the same strategies to promote your land based business, or maybe you also want to promote affiliate programs.

AFFILIATE PROGRAMS

If you want to promote affiliate programs but have no idea where to start, sign up with the affiliate network Commission Junction (http://www.cj.com). Once signed up, review the different programs that are offered.

If you simply want to target affiliate niches that earn the most money, this is what I recommend. These are the top affiliate niches in terms of income. Do remember that more income generally equals more competition.

Dating: The wonderful thing about this industry is that you can create niche-specific websites—for example, Jewish or Christian dating, as well as lesbian or gay dating. They even have lifestyle-type dating websites such as athletic, artistic, travel, etc. You can also target by age or parental status, such as single parents, seniors, etc.

Gambling: Hugely profitable. There's bingo, casino, poker, and sports betting.

Contact Lenses: I would estimate this will shrink with time as more people obtain laser eye surgery, but I knew an affiliate who earned six figures a month from this.

Diet Pills and Health: Herbal products pay up to 50% commission and are very profitable.

Financial: Debt consolidation and payday loans are huge. Debt consolidation, also known as debt management or debt settlement loans, pay on average $30 a lead. Payday loans, also known as cash advances, pay from $30 to $100 a lead.

Flowers and Gift Baskets: I've done relatively well with this niche but the commissions are a bit smaller than I like. The volume of people using these services offers a lot of opportunity. One opportunity that I have seen but never taken is localized searches. For instance, someone in Fort Lauderdale, FL might search for "FT Lauderdale flowers," You could create a website, or pages off a website, for this term. The same would apply for any city.

Travel: I never did very well with this to be honest, but the sky is really the limit. Unfortunately, travel does require more in-depth websites with significant content. The other problem is that Google likes to compete with webmasters and they insert their own content into the search results. Nonetheless, if you can figure out how to monetize travel, the profits can be staggering.

Of course, I do believe that if you can think outside of the box, you can add something to this list

I keep a list of some of my most profitable affiliate programs at http://www.dotaffiliate.com/topaffiliateprograms.html

COMING FULL CIRCLE

I've been doing this for over a decade. It's quite shocking how long it has been. Essentially, everything I did prior to 2008 was for nothing. Nonetheless, the life experience has made me who I am so I wouldn't change it.

I've watched banking affiliates earn six figures a month and they would burn through the cash. All of a sudden, they have a website that no longer ranks well and they can no longer sustain the high life. I urge everyone to be conservative. When you start earning money, save a portion of it. Ensure that you have six-months income in reserve, and only then should you start "going crazy." A lot of people only want to make a couple hundred extra a month, or enough to quit a day job. This is, of course, commendable and achievable.

I do urge that you prioritize your family and health over the internet business. I've seen affiliates live high, only to lose it all to poor health. You only live once and money is not the most important thing. You might need to work hard initially but then you can live the life that you want. For me, I wanted freedom to travel and the freedom to live in the tropics.

I cannot imagine having to work at a regular job. I have been so blessed. Even with all of the initial failures and the frustrations, at the end of the day

I am lucky. I also think that at the end of the day the internet gave me what was important and now I have it.

Over the past year, I have more and more distanced myself from the internet. I bought a significant volume of real estate during the recession. This offers steady, maintenance-free monthly dividends. The end result is that I no longer have to work and yet the affiliate income keeps rolling in.

Since I have over 500 websites, the law of diminishing returns is in effect. The odds of one more website significantly increasing my bottom line is next to none. It's time for me to return to traveling, to increase my volunteering, and to work on things that are important to me. I love having the freedom and flexibility to do this.

When I was a teenager, I wanted to write a book and I abandoned the idea to focus on the internet riches. This is my chance to come full circle. In a way, I have returned to my roots. I started off unhappy with life, living somewhere miserable, and then I took the wrong paths and made mistakes. Now I know better. I initially wanted to help charities by raising money. Now I have the freedom of time to volunteer. That is a wonderful thing. Now I can work on projects that make me happy versus working for money. The most valuable asset one has is time—time to spend with family, time to volunteer, time to enjoy life, and time to be healthy. The internet can afford you that valuable asset.

THE FUTURE

I believe I have given the simplest map to generate internet wealth. Some people might dismiss it as being too simple, but I assume I have proven that simple works. Google had the simplest design, while Yahoo had a confusing and busy layout. The end result was that Google won users because of its simplicity. Simple websites convert the best and, more importantly, are the easiest to create.

I have no web design or programming skills. If you have some of these, you have an unfair advantage over me and others. If you don't have these skills, that's why there are outsourcing sites. Do not allow a lack of skills to get in the way of progress or your dreams. I knew at the beginning that it made more sense to outsource than to learn a skill, and this holds true to this day. Better yet, it is now easier to outsource than ever. If I post a project on elance.com I have 20+ bids within hours.

With outsourcing, make sure you are clear in your demands. Give example websites and specify what images you want. For instance, for a Canadian site, I specify that in the header I want a Canadian flag, the title of the website, and an image that reflects what the content is about.

While I have outlined what works for me now, the internet is forever evolving. There is no avoiding this, but as long as you can learn to adapt and evolve with the times, you can generate a decent income. I bet that you are more committed than I was from 2008 onwards. After all, I was traveling nine months a year and working for three months! And this is the period of time when my income sky rocketed!

The important thing is not the formula. What is important is gaining a nugget of influence from here, as well as other places, and combining it with what you know about the world and then using that to your advantage.

I wish you the best of luck in your future ventures!

TOOLS

Advertising:

http://advertising.yahoo.com — Allows you to advertise on a pay-per-click model on both yahoo.com and bing.com

http://adwords.google.com — Allows you to advertise on a pay-per-click model on google.com. The colored listings on the side and top of Google are all paid listings.

Affiliate Programs:

http://www.clickbank.com — I know of many webmasters that do well with this affiliate network but I never focused on it much. I am only including it because I do believe that it has potential. This is for 100% "virtual" products, such as e-books. On a good note, you can get paid up to 75% in commission. On the downside, the products that you can promote are generally of poor quality.

http://www.cj.com — The largest affiliate network in the world. You can promote almost anything other than adult material and gambling

http://www.dotaffiliate.com/topaffiliateprograms.html — The website that I have created to complement this book. I keep a list of my current highest-earning affiliate programs here.

http://www.gamblingaffiliateprograms.net — If you want to promote casinos, poker rooms, bingo halls, or sports books.

http://www.healthaffiliateprograms.com — If you want to promote diet pills, acne treatments, or other health products, this lists the top affiliate programs.

https://www.google.com/adsense — If you have a website idea and cannot find an affiliate program that would fit on your website, sign up for Google AdSense. They will then offer ads that are targeted to the content on your website. I found that ordinary affiliate programs were SIGNIFICANTLY more profitable to AdSense and I would recommend AdSense ONLY if you cannot find a regular affiliate program.

Charity:

These are websites that allow visitors to click daily to sponsor free donations to important charities.

http://www.thehungersite.com — Helps feed starving children.

http://www.thebreastcancersite.com — Helps fund research to fight breast cancer.

http://www.theanimalrescuesite.com — Helps domesticated animals in need of assistance.

http://www.theautismsite.com — Offers free therapy to those who suffer from autism.

http://www.thechildhealthsite.com — Offers free health care to children who qualify for it.

http://www.therainforestsite.com — Buys rainforests for conservation purposes.

http://www.theliterarysite.com — Buys books for poor children.

http://www.ecologyfund.com – Offers various options to conserve land and natural resources.

Content Writers:

I use these resources when I need to have content written for my websites. Normally, I write the index (main page) myself and outsource the content for the internal pages.

http://www.textbroker.com — I love how simple this website is to use. You post the content that you need written, including how many words you need, and you receive articles normally within 48 hours. The quality you receive depends on how much you are willing to pay.

http://www.writeraccess.com — Similar to the item above, but I have used only a few times.

Directories:

It's impossible to keep a current list of directories in a book format. Please visit this page on my website to see the recommended list:

http://www.dotaffiliate.com/directories.html

Domain Names:

http://www.moniker.com — I use this registrar to register domain names, but there are a ton of different registrars out there.

http://www.onlinenic.com — Another registrar I use.

http://www.sedo.com — A marketplace to buy and sell domain names.

File Transfer Protocol (FTP):

This tool is used to upload or download content from your computer to the server on which your website resides. I tried numerous FTP clients in the beginning but then I found a FREE client which is an add-on to Firefox.

fireftp.mozdev.org — This FREE FTP is an add-on to the Firefox browser and is compatible with all operating systems. After using this, I never went back to another FTP client.

Keyword Research:

https://adwords.google.com/select/KeywordToolExternal — This is what I use. It is completely free.

http://www.wordtracker.com — Has a free option and a paid option. I have only ever used the free option.

Marketing:

http://www.prweb.com — Professional press-release writing and submission that is worthwhile if you are willing to pay the associated cost. This is preferred if you actually expect newspapers and large websites to pick up your press release. This is a far more effective service than WL Marketing, but much more expensive.

http://www.submitedge.com — Offers various marketing tools to generate links to your website. Some of them might be frowned upon by Google, so you do risk having your website banned or penalized. I only use this if buying directory links and WL Marketing is not enough to get me ranking high.

http://www.wlmarketing.com — Cheap article writing (to submit to websites that post articles), press releases, social bookmarking, and submissions to "free" directories. The writing is not very good, so you might want to consider writing your own articles and press releases and just use the submission service.

Search Engine Optimization:

I prefer to study search results to learn from them, but sometimes you need to gather information from others in the business. These are some of the websites I visit occasionally:

http://www.searchenginewatch.com — They are always on top of new changes that involve SEO.

http://www.seobook.com — I am not a member but I do read the blog.

http://www.seochat.com — One of the most popular forums in the industry; a lot of information but information overload and misinformation is always a problem.

http://www.webmasterworld.com — A huge forum, and they have webmaster conferences that are fun to attend.

Statistics:

http://www.statcounter.com — A free counter that will allow you to track website visitors from visitor location, browsers used, operating systems used, as well as the search engine query that was used to locate your website.

Web Design:

http://www.freelancer.com — Outsource your websites here. Post a project and have designers and programmers bidding on your project.

http://www.elance.com — The original outsourcing website that is owned by ebay.com. Similar to the above.

http://www.guru.com — Very popular, but the service I have personally used the least.

http://www.99designs.com — Similar to the above outsourcing websites but of higher cost and quality. The difference is that you post a design project and offer a monetary reward. Designers submit mockups and you pick the best design and award the winner a prize. I use this service for important designs. For instance, I paid $499 to start a competition for this book cover.

Webhosting:

This is who I use, depending on what market I am targeting:

http://www.hostgator.com — Extremely cheap; I use this for American websites.

http://www.canadianwebhosting.com — This is who I use for my Canadian websites.

http://www.quadrahosting.com.au — This is who I use for my Australian websites.

http://www.hostroute.com — I use them for my UK websites.

This list is far from comprehensive; it's just who I have the most positive experience with.

About the Author:

Antoine Walker lives in the Cayman Islands. He loves to travel, especially to secluded islands and undeveloped destinations. This is his first published book. You may reach him at http://www.dotaffiliate.com

www.ingramcontent.com/pod-product-compliance
Lightning Source LLC
Chambersburg PA
CBHW061510180526
45171CB00001B/113